Montague Island *Mysteries*

and Other Logic Puzzles

R. Wayne Schmittberger

PUZZLE WRIGHT PRESS
New York

An Imprint of Sterling Publishing Co., Inc.
1166 Avenue of the Americas
New York, NY 10036

PUZZLEWRIGHT PRESS and the distinctive Puzzlewright Press logo
are registered trademarks of Sterling Publishing Co., Inc.

ISBN 978-1-4549-1811-0

Distributed in Canada by Sterling Publishing Co., Inc.
c/o Canadian Manda Group, 664 Annette Street
Toronto, Ontario, Canada M6S 2C8
Distributed in the United Kingdom by GMC Distribution Services
Castle Place, 166 High Street, Lewes, East Sussex, England BN7 1XU
Distributed in Australia by NewSouth Books
45 Beach Street, Coogee, NSW 2034, Australia

For information about custom editions, special sales, and premium
and corporate purchases, please contact Sterling Special Sales
at 800-805-5489 or specialsales@sterlingpublishing.com.

Manufactured in China

2 4 6 8 10 9 7 5 3

www.sterlingpublishing.com
www.puzzlewright.com

Contents

Introduction

During my 35 years at *Games* magazine, I edited, solved, and constructed a wide variety of puzzles, and logic puzzles were always a favorite. My initial idea for this book came from the genre of mystery party games: I imagined a set of recurring characters who get together to act out roles in mystery stories while trying to solve those very mysteries. Then, in trying to figure out how best to make puzzles based on such a format, I realized that those mysteries would work best as part of a larger world in which they and other logic puzzles exist naturally—much in the way that songs in a musical spring up naturally when the play's subject is the making of a musical.

This book will take you to Montague Island, home of a wealthy couple who are passionate about playing games, solving puzzles, and creating puzzles for others to solve. During the warm months each year, they invite several guests to come to their island every other weekend to engage in a variety of activities, including acting out parts in mysteries that the Montagues have created. Everything the guests do on the island, from playing in game tournaments to taking part in a season-long puzzle-solving competition, provides new material for a book of logic puzzles that the Montagues are compiling.

The reader sees the island for the first time through the eyes of Taylor, a guest who has a secret reason for being there. That secret will gradually be revealed, bringing with it another mystery to solve.

Some of the elements in the book are based on personal experiences. Montague Street in Brooklyn Heights, where I would often visit my grandparents as a child, is the source of the name in the title. The island setting was inspired by Gardiner's Island, a privately owned island between Long Island's two eastern peninsulas, which was visible from the place I worked during three summers of my college years. And the games mentioned in some of the puzzles are games I have played, sometimes extensively.

In this book you'll find some traditional logic puzzles that can be solved with a grid, unconventional puzzles that require special methods, and mysteries in which guilty suspects may make false statements to mislead the solver. May you enjoy your visit.

—R. Wayne Schmittberger

Welcome to the Island

You wait at a dock as the cabin cruiser approaches the South Carolina coast. On this late Friday afternoon in May, you mentally prepare yourself for the first of a dozen trips you are committed to take to the island between now and October.

The other people assembled on the dock, three men and three women, know one another. They were all regular visitors to the island last year. You've become a new guest for a reason you must keep secret. You'll be using the name Taylor.

The cabin cruiser pulls alongside the end of the dock, and a casually dressed middle-aged man who introduces himself as Alistair invites you aboard. Someone else, unseen, is piloting the boat.

Montague Island lies nearly four miles from the mainland. From the dock, the island's only discernible detail is the lighthouse on the island's western end.

The trip from the mainland takes less than half an hour. The lighthouse is on your left as the marina comes into view. Soon you see several motorboats and small sailboats tied up to buoys within an area about half the size of a football field, flanked by two docks.

You and the other passengers disembark and are led past a boathouse onto a gravel path that forks in three directions. You follow Alistair onto the middle path, which winds gently uphill through dense woods. After a few hundred yards, the path opens up to reveal a one-and-a-half-century-old, three-story mansion. In front of the house are gardens, and to the right are a greenhouse and shed. Beyond the mansion and to its right, a cottage is just visible in the distance.

Alistair leads everyone onto the front porch, through the front door, and into a foyer. He asks everyone to remove their shoes. All the guests comply without comment and are ushered into an enormous lounge furnished with enough sofas, armchairs, and tables to accommodate several dozen people. Display cases in two corners of the room contain a variety of small sculptures, and one wall is decorated with colorful tapestries depicting medieval scenes. Through an open door on the other side of the foyer, you can see several paintings hanging on a wall.

"Dinner will be served in one hour," Alistair announces. "That should give you all time to solve a puzzle that will tell you where you are to sit tonight. In the meantime, I'll take your orders for something to drink." Alistair hands each guest a piece of paper, shown on the next page.

Meet the Guests

Tonight, your hosts Gordon and Nina Montague will be sitting at the ends of the dining room table, as shown. The seven guests—Beth, Charles, David, Frank, Jessica, Karen, and Taylor—will be seated along the sides of the table, four on one side and three on the other. From the clues below, can you determine each guest's home state (California, Florida, Kentucky, Montana, New York, Texas, or Wisconsin) and the place where each guest will sit (as labeled Seat 1 through Seat 7 in the diagram)?

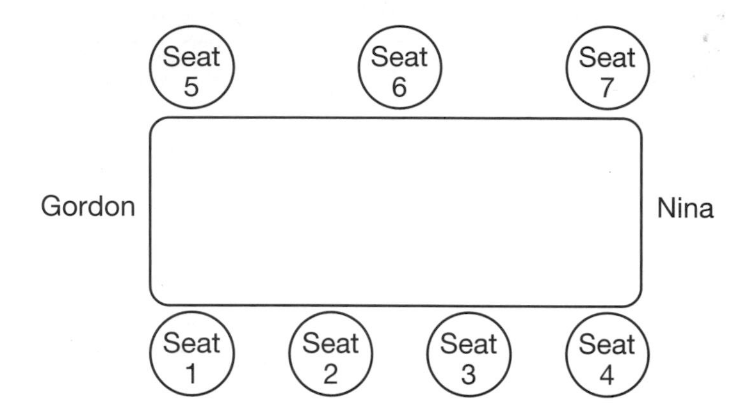

1. The only two left-handed guests will be seated at corners, to the immediate rights of Gordon and Nina Montague.
2. The two guests who will sit next to the guest from Montana are from Florida and Wisconsin, and are both right-handed.
3. Both Taylor, who is not from Montana, and the guest from California are right-handed.
4. Frank and Jessica, who are both right-handed, will sit on different sides of the table.
5. The guest from New York is right-handed.
6. Charles and the guest from Florida will sit next to left-handed guests.
7. Frank and the guest from California will sit next to the Montagues.
8. Beth will sit on the same side of the table as the guest from Texas, who is not Karen.

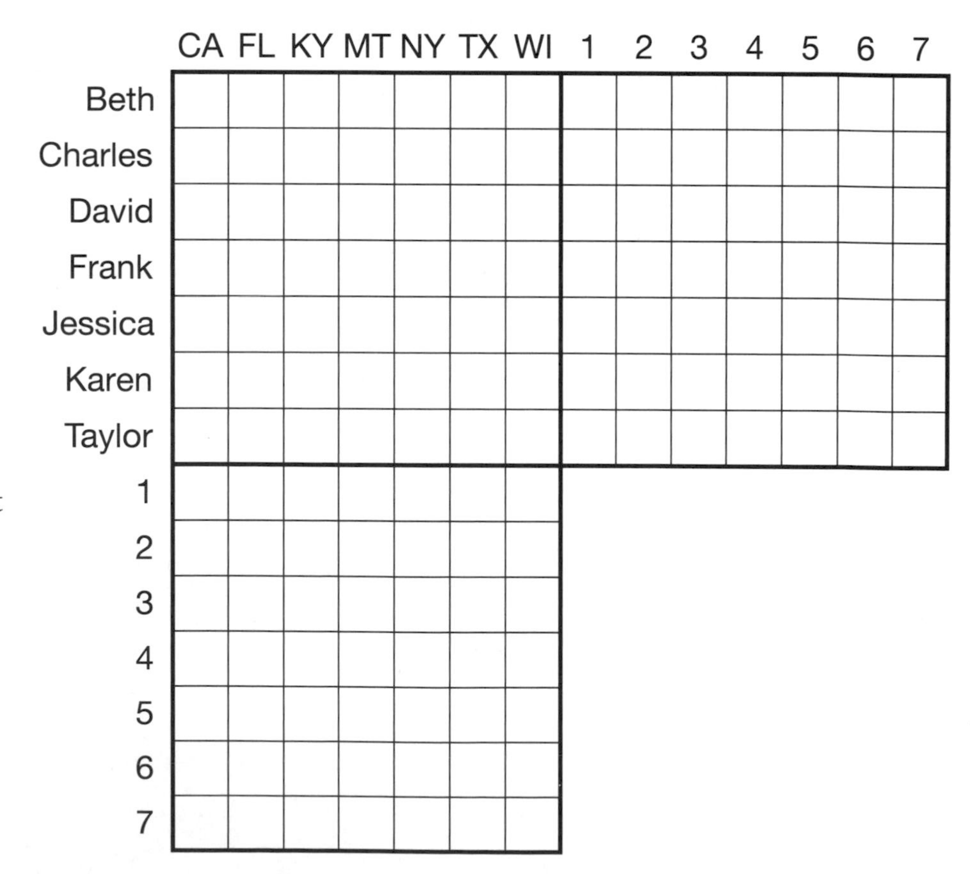

The dining room and the lounge are connected by a double door. The heavy oak dining table and ornate brass chandelier are very much what you expected. Place cards showing the guests' names are face down; but having solved the puzzle presented earlier by Alistair, all the guests go to their appointed seats without reading the cards and only need to wait for a moment before Gordon and Nina Montague, dressed in semiformal attire, enter the room.

The Montagues appear to be in their mid-forties, but you happen to know that Gordon is actually 55 and Nina 51. You also know that Gordon amassed his fortune as an entrepreneur (or as some would say, corporate raider), while Nina had an early acting career followed by a successful turn as an attorney and high-profile litigator. Both are now retired.

Gordon speaks first. "Nina and I welcome you to a new season on our island. This weekend, as you know, and in eleven more weekends over the next few months, each of you will be asked to solve puzzles, play competitive games, and sometimes play the role of a character in a mystery story in which a crime has been committed. When there is such a mystery, as there will be tomorrow, you will become detectives whose goal is to solve the crime. At least one of you will be the person who committed the crime; but even if your character is guilty, you will not know this until you have solved the mystery like the other players.

"What a complete solution to a mystery puzzle consists of will vary from one of our stories to another. Besides being asked to name the guilty party or parties, for example, you may have to locate stolen property or determine the motive for the crime.

"After dinner, each of you will be shown to your room. By sunrise, an envelope will have been slipped under each of your doors, containing specific instructions you will need for tomorrow's mystery.

"As those who have been here before know, we ask our guests to call us, as well as each other, only by first names. You will use your own first names in all mystery games, but other facts about you, such as your occupation or your favorite book, may be fictitious facts made up for purposes of a particular story.

"The most important thing in your instructions is the key statement or statements that you must provide to other players when they question you. Such statements will always be true when spoken by an innocent character, but may or may not be true when spoken by a guilty party. You may embellish the phrasing of a key statement, provided you are very careful not to change its essence."

Nina Montague continues the orientation. "Breakfast will be served at 7:30 tomorrow morning. After that, each of you will go to a different location on the island by 10 A.M., as directed by your individual instructions. After that you may go wherever you wish, except that all of you are required to be here for lunch at noon and dinner at 7 P.M., to ensure that everyone has an opportunity to question everyone else and learn their key statements.

"Your primary goal in tomorrow's activity, of course, is to enjoy solving the mystery. But a secondary goal is to solve the mystery as quickly as you can. The first, second, and third of you to correctly provide a solution to this weekend's mystery will be assured of earning 20, 15, and 10 points respectively out of the 100 points we divide among the guests at the end of each weekend, based on how well they performed in whatever puzzle-solving and game competitions took place. On the final weekend, the guest with the highest point total will be awarded a select item from our art collection.

"When you have a solution, you may present it to Gordon, me, or any of our staff. We will verify that it is a correct and complete solution, and note the time you gave it to us. Of course, this means it is in your interest to get statements from everyone else as quickly as possible. By 'everyone else,' I don't just mean the other guests. Gordon and I, as well as our six full-time employees who live here, will all participate as characters in most of our mystery stories and will have statements to give you. When you question Gordon or me or one of our staff, you can rely on our statements to be true. If Gordon and I have designed the mystery correctly, the statements by us, our staff, and all the guests, taken together, will suffice to solve the mystery.

"You have met Alistair, our head of staff; our other employees who live here are chef Evelyn, gardener Grant, nurse Lyle, secretary Molly, and housekeeper Sandy.

"If ever any of the rules Gordon and I have just explained change for a particular mystery, we will let you know."

Before retiring for the night, Gordon hands out envelopes to everyone, saying, "Here's a little after-dinner warm-up puzzle." (The puzzle appears on the next page.) You decide to take that puzzle to your room to solve, but not before looking around the mansion's first floor and surveying the grounds outdoors to get a better idea of their layouts (shown below).

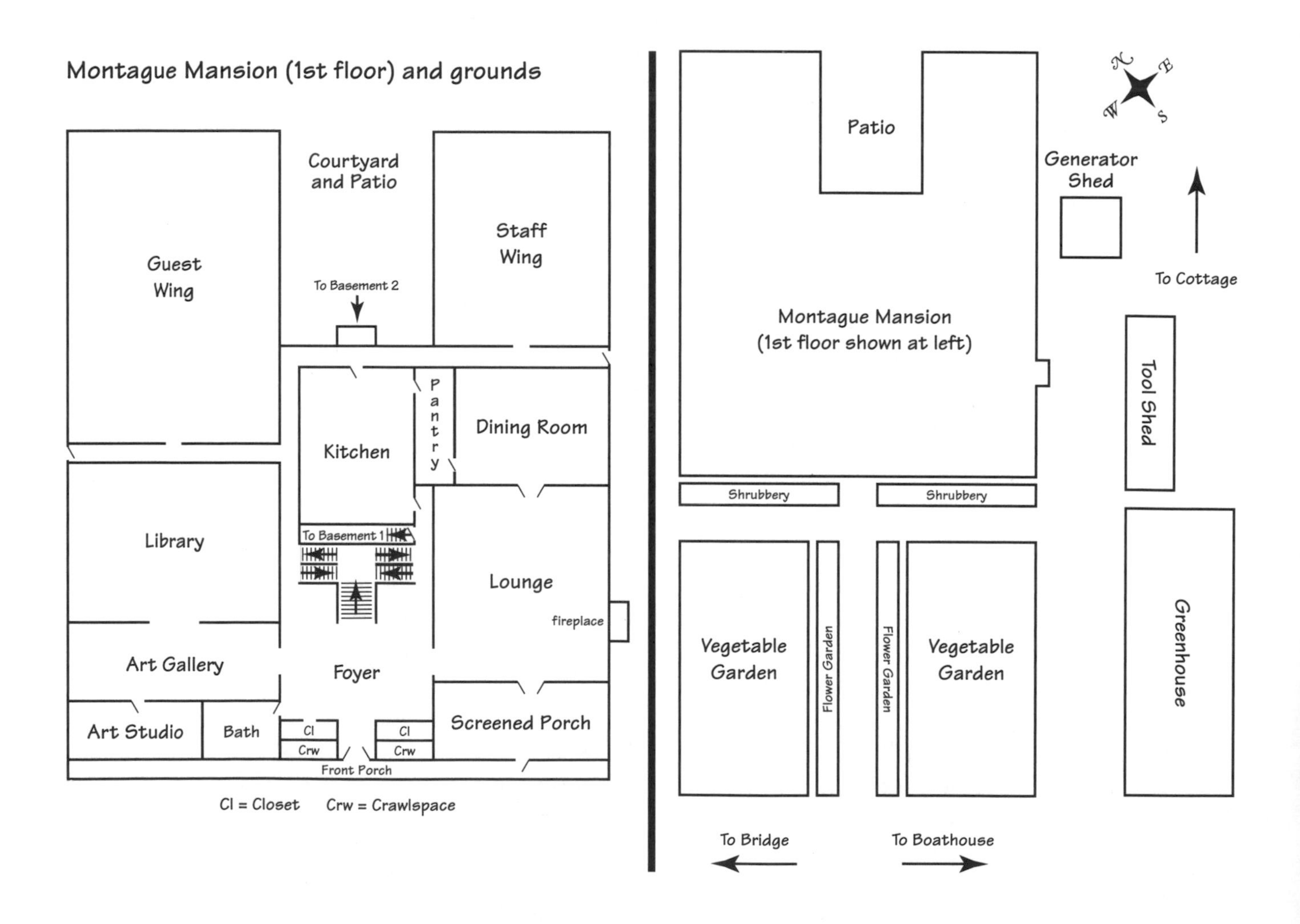

True-False Test

Each envelope handed out by Gordon Montague contains two playing cards and a piece of paper with two statements on it.

"Don't show your cards to anyone else," Gordon warns, "but do reveal the two statements on your papers. The puzzle is to determine the suits of all the players' cards without looking at any cards but your own.

"There are two things you need to know. First, each of your papers contains one true statement and one false statement. Either the true statement or the false statement may come first. And second, the suits of the 14 cards in the guests' hands comprise four clubs, four diamonds, three hearts, and three spades."

Here are the guests' statements. Can you determine the suits of all the players' cards?

Beth:
I have a club and a spade.
I have a heart and a spade.

Charles:
I have a diamond and a heart.
I have at least one spade.

David:
I have a club and a spade.
I have exactly one spade.

Frank:
I have a club and a heart.
I have a club and a spade.

Jessica:
I have a club and a spade.
One of my cards is a spade, and my other card is not a diamond.

Karen:
I have no diamonds.
I have at least one spade.

Taylor:
I have a club and a heart.
I have two cards of the same suit.

The Missing Painting

An envelope that was pushed under your door during the night contains this piece of paper:

> **MYSTERY PUZZLE**
>
> **Instructions for Taylor**
>
> During the night, a priceless painting disappeared from the gallery on the first floor of the mansion. At 10 A.M., be in the garden in front of the house. After that, you are free to look around the island and talk to other players. If you should happen to find the painting, you must leave it where it is.
>
> **Required for a complete solution**
>
> Locate the painting and determine who stole it. Keep in mind that a statement by a guilty party may or may not be true.
>
> **Statement you are to give to other players**
>
> *I am an attorney, and I started in the garden.*
> *If the painting is at the windmill, then Jessica is guilty.*

Over the course of the next day, you interview everyone and compile the following list of statements:

Statements by the Montagues:

1. Gordon: The seven guests' occupations are: attorney, banker, composer, decorator, entrepreneur, filmmaker, and gerontologist. The thief acted alone.
2. Nina: The painting was stolen between midnight and 6 A.M. Either the painting is still somewhere inside the mansion, or the thief hid it at one of four other locations: the boathouse, the cottage, the lighthouse, or the windmill.

Statements by the staff:

3. Alistair: At 10 A.M. the guests started from seven different locations: the boathouse, cottage, garden, lighthouse, mansion, pond, and windmill.
4. Evelyn: If the entrepreneur is innocent, the painting is no longer in the mansion.
5. Grant: The painting is not at the location where the gerontologist started.
6. Lyle: Karen is the decorator.
7. Molly: At 10 A.M. the entrepreneur, filmmaker, and gerontologist started at the cottage, mansion, and pond, in some order.
8. Sandy: If Charles is guilty, the painting is not in the cottage.

Statements by the guests:

9. Beth: I'm a banker, and I started at the windmill. The painting is not there.
10. Charles: I'm a gerontologist, and I did not start at either the mansion or the pond.
11. David: The painting is not in the boathouse or the place where I started.
12. Frank: I'm not the entrepreneur, but I do know where the entrepreneur started, and it was not the mansion.
13. Jessica: The painting is not hidden where I started, which was neither the mansion nor the pond.
14. Karen: I started at the lighthouse. The painting is not hidden in either the boathouse, the lighthouse, or the mansion.
15. Taylor: I am an attorney, and I started in the garden. If the painting is at the windmill, then Jessica is guilty.

	attorney	banker	composer	decorator	entrepreneur	filmmaker	gerontologist	boathouse	cottage	garden	lighthouse	mansion	pond	windmill
Beth														
Charles														
David														
Frank														
Jessica														
Karen														
Taylor														

	attorney	banker	composer	decorator	entrepreneur	filmmaker	gerontologist
boathouse							
cottage							
garden							
lighthouse							
mansion							
pond							
windmill							

The Guest Rooms

Nearly two weeks after the first puzzle weekend of the year, the seven guests—Beth, Charles, David, Frank, Jessica, Karen, and Taylor—are back on a Friday evening. Over dinner, the Montagues outline the events they have planned for the weekend. Afterward, the Montagues show their guests a floor plan of the guest wing's three floors, with its 15 guest rooms labeled 1A through 3E, and explain that it will be used in the following puzzle in the book they are working on:

From the floor plan shown at right and the following clues, can you determine which guest is staying in which guest room?

1. Each of the seven guests is in a different room; the other eight guest rooms are empty.
2. At least two guests are staying on each of the three floors.
3. Beth, David, Jessica, and Taylor each have a room with a closet that is adjacent to the closet of a room occupied by another guest.
4. Karen's room is on the same floor and the same side of the hall as the room of one of the two guests whose rooms have a closet that is adjacent to the area designated as "crawlspace" on the floor plan.
5. Beth's room and Jessica's room are on different floors.
6. When walking directly from her own room to Karen's room, Jessica will pass exactly twice as many guest room doorways (counting doorways of both occupied and unoccupied guest rooms) as Beth will pass when walking directly from her own room to Charles's room. (The doorways of the starting and destination rooms do not count as being "passed" during a walk. Only guest room doors count, not bathroom or storage room doors.)
7. David's room's floor is one level higher than Frank's.
8. At least one of the D rooms is occupied.

	1A	1B	1C	1D	1E	2A	2B	2C	2D	2E	3A	3B	3C	3D	3E
Beth															
Charles															
David															
Frank															
Jessica															
Karen															
Taylor															

Guest Wing

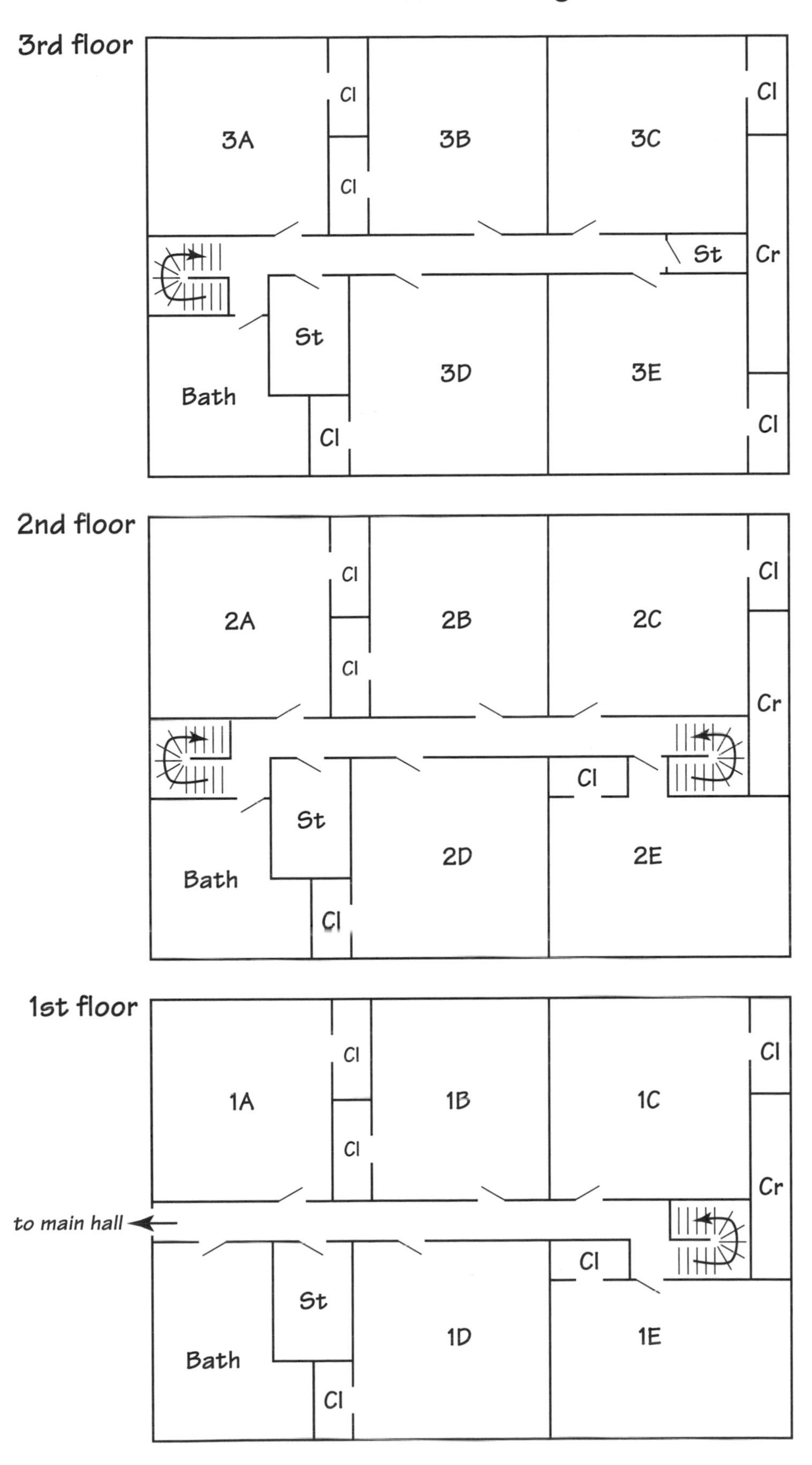

Cl = Closet St = Storage Cr = Crawlspace

An Evening of Diplomacy

After dinner, the Montagues invite their seven guests to play the classic board game Diplomacy, which was invented by Allan B. Calhamer and first published in the 1950s. In the game, each player assumes the role of a European nation just before the start of World War I. The object is to maneuver armies and navies to capture at least half the supply centers on the board, which is a stylized map of Europe. The key to the game is making secret deals with other players between turns to support one another's planned attacks or defenses, but players are free to break those deals whenever it best suits their purpose. The most conniving player will typically win by deceiving the others into believing that he or she is no threat to them, until it is too late.

The game lasts well into the night. From the following observations made by the Montagues and their staff, can you determine which of the guests played which country, and what their order of finish was from first (best) through seventh (worst)?

Note: The first player eliminated ranked seventh, the next player eliminated ranked sixth, and so on. After a player achieved victory, any players not already eliminated were ranked according to how many pieces they had left on the board, making it possible to rank all the players from 1 through 7.

1. Russia finished better than Germany, which in turn did better than Turkey.
2. Austria-Hungary outlasted England, England survived longer than France, and France was still playing after Italy was eliminated.
3. Beth placed higher than David, who did better than Karen, who in turn did better than Charles.
4. Frank did better than Taylor, who did better than Jessica.
5. David finished two places better than Italy but two places worse than Russia.
6. England finished two places better than Karen but two places worse than Frank.
7. Germany did not end up in second or third place, but finished one place either above or below Taylor.
8. Jessica did not play Turkey.

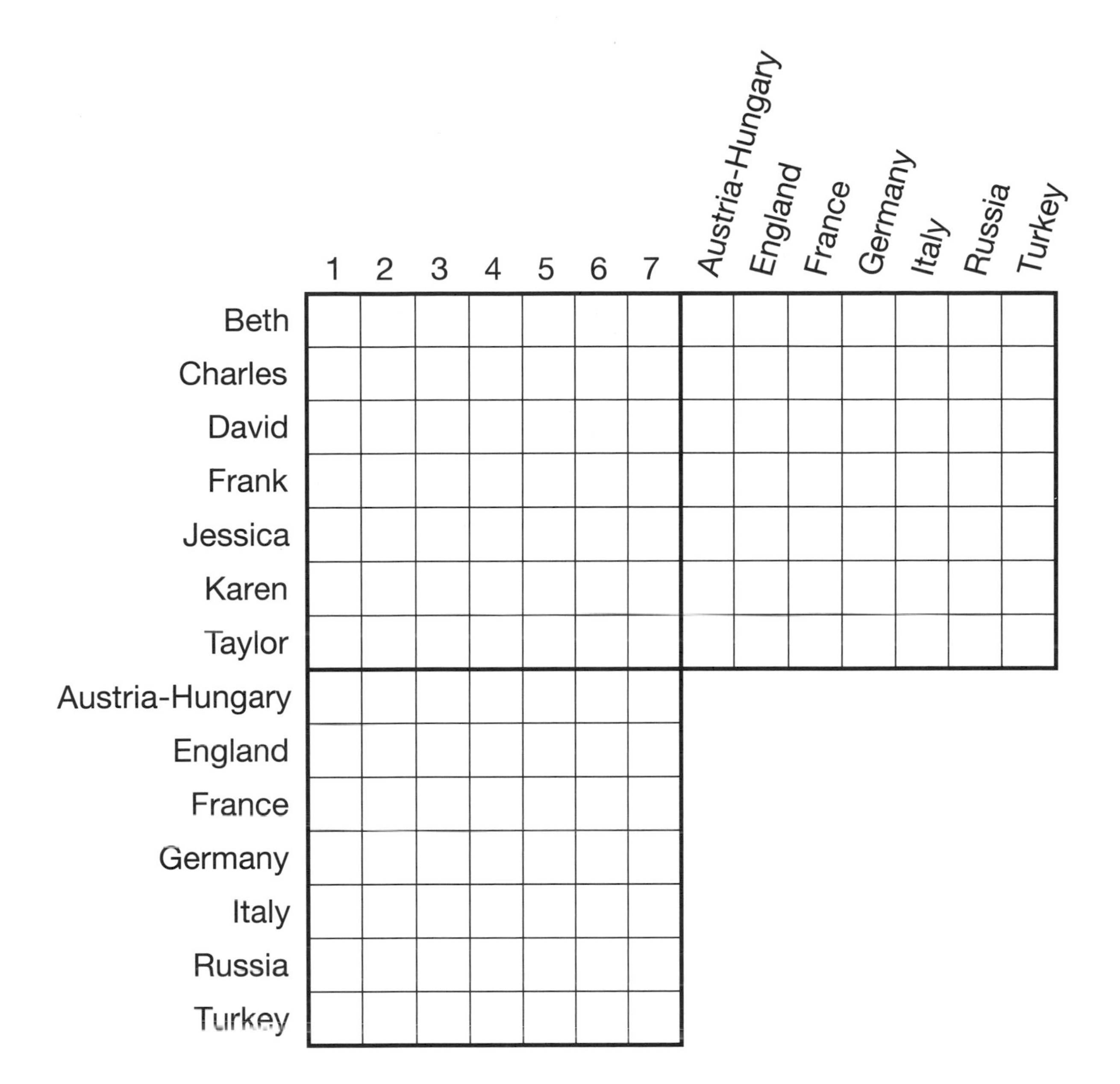
1
2
3
4
5
6
7
Austria-Hungary
England
France
Germany
Italy
Russia
Turkey
Beth
Charles
David
Frank
Jessica
Karen
Taylor
Austria-Hungary
England
France
Germany
Italy
Russia
Turkey

In the Library

During the Saturday lunch that follows the Friday night Diplomacy game, each guest is given an envelope with preliminary instructions for the day's mystery puzzle. They state that a crime will be discovered sometime this afternoon. They also tell each guest to be in the library during a specific time period after lunch, and to all come to the lounge at 4:30. In the lounge, you receive further written instructions:

MYSTERY PUZZLE

Instructions for Taylor

The body of Grant, the gardener, was found this afternoon in the greenhouse next to the garden. He had been fatally stabbed. A knife with traces of blood was found in the library. (Don't be alarmed—the "murder" is just part of the game, and Grant will be fully "recovered" by our next mystery game.)

Required for a complete solution

Name the guilty party or parties; and, as corroborating evidence, determine the time that each guest was in the library and what magazine each guest subscribes to. Keep in mind that in all mystery puzzles, the killer(s) may lie when questioned.

Statement you are to give to other players

I visited the library from just after lunch until 1:30. Each guest including myself subscribes to a different magazine, their titles being Courts Illustrated, Ferret Fancy, Feud & Whine, Field & Dream, Height Watchers, Popular Séance, *and* Vanity Hair.

By the next day you have interviewed everyone and compiled the following list of statements:

Statements by the Montagues:

1. Gordon: The killer acted alone. Grant had discovered that the guest was a wanted criminal, but he was silenced before he could pass that information to anyone. Beth, Frank, Jessica, and Taylor subscribe to *Courts Illustrated, Ferret Fancy, Feud & Whine*, and *Vanity Hair*, in some order.

2. Nina: Only one of the following three facts is true: Charles subscribes to *Field & Dream*; David subscribes to *Height Watchers*; Karen subscribes to *Popular Séance*. And only one of these other four facts is true: Beth subscribes to *Courts Illustrated*; Frank subscribes to *Ferret Fancy*; Jessica subscribes to *Vanity Hair*; Taylor subscribes to *Feud & Whine*.

Statements by the staff:

3. Alistair: No more than two guests were ever in the library at the same time. The knife found in the library could only have been placed there between 2:30 and 3:30.

4. Evelyn: If Beth subscribes to *Ferret Fancy*, then Taylor subscribes to *Vanity Hair*. If Taylor subscribes to *Vanity Hair*, then Karen does not subscribe to *Height Watchers*.

5. Lyle: If Charles subscribes to *Popular Séance*, then Karen subscribes to *Height Watchers*.

6. Molly: If Taylor subscribes to *Ferret Fancy*, then Jessica subscribes to *Courts Illustrated*.

7. Sandy: Only one of the following statements is true: Charles subscribes to *Popular Séance*; Jessica subscribes to *Courts Illustrated*; Taylor subscribes to *Ferret Fancy*.

Statements by the guests:

8. Beth: I was in the library between 3:30 and 4:30 with the guest who subscribes to *Height Watchers*.

9. Charles: I was in the library between 3:30 and 4:30 with the guest who subscribes to *Feud & Whine*.

10. David: I was in the library between 3:30 and 4:30. The guest who subscribes to *Field & Dream* was in the library at that time.

11. Frank: I was in the library between 1:30 and 2:30.

12. Jessica: I was in the library between 2:30 and 3:30. One other guest, who does not subscribe to either *Feud & Whine* or *Height Watchers*, was in the library at the same time.

13. Karen: I was in the library between 1:30 and 2:30.

14. Taylor: I visited the library from just after lunch until 1:30. Each guest including myself subscribes to a different magazine, their titles being *Courts Illustrated, Ferret Fancy, Feud & Whine, Field & Dream, Height Watchers, Popular Séance*, and *Vanity Hair*.

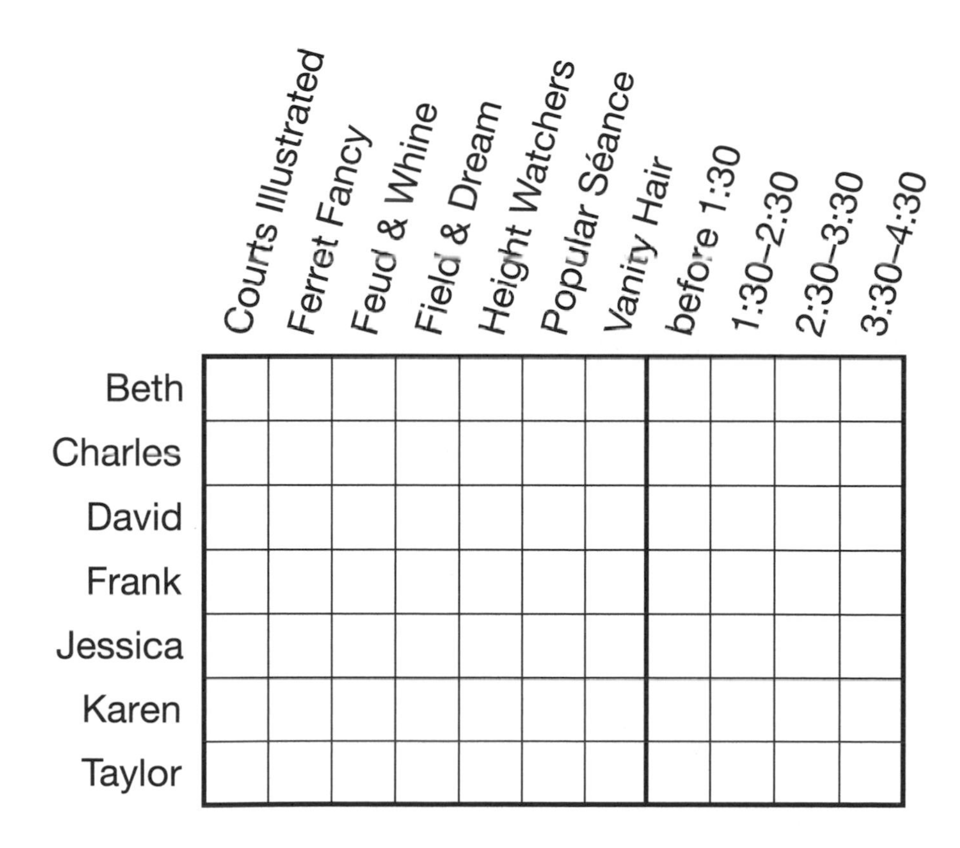

Movie Poll

On Friday evening of the third puzzle weekend, Gordon Montague holds up a poster-size list of eleven well-known movie titles and hands out paper and pencil to each of the seven guests—Beth, Charles, David, Frank, Jessica, Karen, and Taylor.

"I'm conducting an unscientific poll," Gordon explains. "I'd like each of you to please choose the three movies on this list that you like best and write their titles on a piece of paper, along with your name. The order in which you list them makes no difference. I'll collect your lists in a little while to tabulate the results, which I'll use as the subject of a new puzzle."

Later that evening, after looking over the lists, Gordon Montague makes the following statements:

1. Two films appeared on four different lists, six films appeared on just one list each, and the other films appeared on either two or three lists.
2. Lists were given scores equal to the number of times that each of its films appeared on other guests' lists. For example, a guest who listed one film that appeared on three other lists, a second film that appeared on just one other guest's list, and another film that was on no other list, would earn a score of 3 + 1 + 0 = 4. The highest score was 8, achieved by just one list, while two lists tied for the lowest score with 2 apiece. The sum of the scores of all seven lists was 34.
3. Besides the two lists that scored 2, the only tie was between two lists with odd-numbered scores.
4. Jessica's and Taylor's lists had one film in common, as did the lists of Charles and Frank.
5. Frank's list included exactly one film listed by no one else, and the same was true of Karen's list.
6. Taylor listed two films that no one else did, and Taylor's list's score was 4 points lower than David's.
7. Karen's list scored more than 2 points.
8. Beth's list included at least one film that appeared on no one else's list.

The problem now posed by Gordon Montague is: What was the score of each guest's list?

	Scores							Movies by Number of Times Listed										
	8	7	6	5	4	3	2	M4	M4	M_	M_	M_	M1	M1	M1	M1	M1	M1
Beth																		
Charles																		
David																		
Frank																		
Jessica																		
Karen																		
Taylor																		

Uncommon Knowledge

The seven guests have a variety of interests and talents, which the Montagues have noted and used to make a puzzle for the book they are working on. Each guest devotes a substantial amount of time to collecting one of the following items, about which he or she is an expert: baseball cards, classic cars, comic books, decoy ducks, perfume bottles, souvenir spoons, and toby jugs; and each guest speaks one of the following foreign languages: Dutch, French, Japanese, Portuguese, Russian, Spanish, and Tagalog. No two guests have the same type of collection or speak the same foreign language.

From the following clues, can you match each guest to his or her collection and foreign language?

1. The collectors of baseball cards, classic cars, and toby jugs speak French, Japanese, and Tagalog, in some combination.
2. Charles, Frank, and Karen speak Dutch, French, and Russian, in some combination.
3. David, Jessica, and Taylor collect baseball cards, souvenir spoons, and toby jugs, in some combination.
4. Beth either speaks Spanish or collects decoy ducks, but not both.
5. Charles either speaks French or collects comic books, but not both.
6. David either speaks Japanese or collects baseball cards, but not both.
7. Jessica either speaks Spanish or collects baseball cards, but not both.
8. Karen either speaks Russian or collects comic books, but not both.
9. Taylor either speaks Tagalog or collects toby jugs, but not both.
10. Frank neither speaks Russian nor collects classic cars.
11. If Charles collects classic cars, David does not speak Japanese.

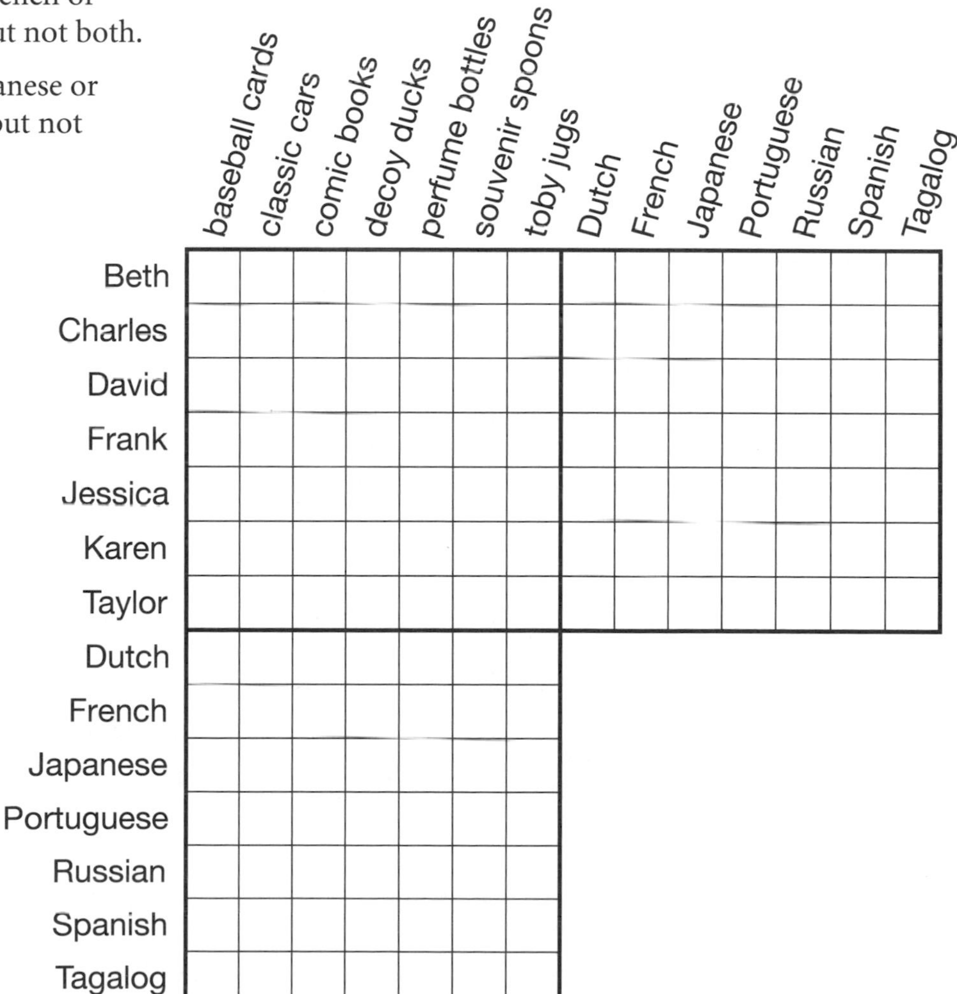

A Brief Tour

An envelope you receive late Friday night contains a map of the island and some instructions.

Instructions for Taylor

You and the other six guests will all take walks around the island tomorrow morning. Be in the dining room at 7 A.M. to have breakfast with the other guests. Guests will begin their walks at seven different times; your starting time will be 8:20. You are to follow your appointed route, reaching each location no more than a minute before or after the scheduled time. From the mansion, you are to visit the following locations in order, adjusting your speed as necessary (watches will be provided if needed) so that you use the indicated number of minutes between each pair of locations:

Leave mansion: 8:20
Walk from mansion to bridge: 10 minutes
Walk from bridge to pond: 10 minutes
Walk from pond to old well: 10 minutes
Walk from old well to sea caves: 10 minutes
Stay at sea caves: 15 minutes
Walk from sea caves to old well: 10 minutes
Walk from old well to pond: 10 minutes
Walk from pond to bridge: 10 minutes
Walk from bridge to mansion: 10 minutes
Return time: 9:55

Saturday at lunch, after all the guests—Beth, Charles, David, Frank, Jessica, Karen, and Taylor—are back from their walks, the Montagues and their staff provide the following information and then pose a question.

1. The guests left the Mansion at seven different times: 8:00, 8:10, 8:20, 8:30, 8:40, 8:50, and 9:00.
2. Of the six guests other than Taylor, two went around the northern loop of paths—mansion, bridge, windmill, old well, pond, bridge, mansion—but traveled in opposite directions from one another after reaching the bridge. Two went around the southern loop of paths—mansion, bridge, pond, old well, Lookout Point, boathouse, mansion—but walked in opposite directions. And two followed the outer loop of paths—mansion, bridge, windmill, old well, Lookout Point, boathouse, mansion—but went in opposite directions.
3. Within a few seconds, the number of minutes each guest took to travel between each pair of locations (walking in either direction) was always as follows:

between mansion and bridge: 10
between bridge and pond: 10
between pond and old well: 10
between bridge and windmill: 30
between windmill and old well: 25
between old well and sea caves (only Taylor used this path): 10
between old well and Lookout Point: 15
between Lookout Point and boathouse: 45
between boathouse and mansion: 10

4. Frank reached the old well later than Charles but earlier than Beth.
5. David left the mansion 10 minutes after Jessica. The two passed each other, walking in opposite directions, just as they reached Lookout Point.
6. David and Karen reached the pond at the same time, walking in opposite directions.
7. Taylor left at 8:20, took the quickest route to the sea caves, spent 15 minutes there, and came directly back to the mansion. No one else visited the old well more than once.
8. Frank arrived back at the mansion 10 minutes after Beth.

The puzzle to be solved is: In what order did the guests visit the old well?

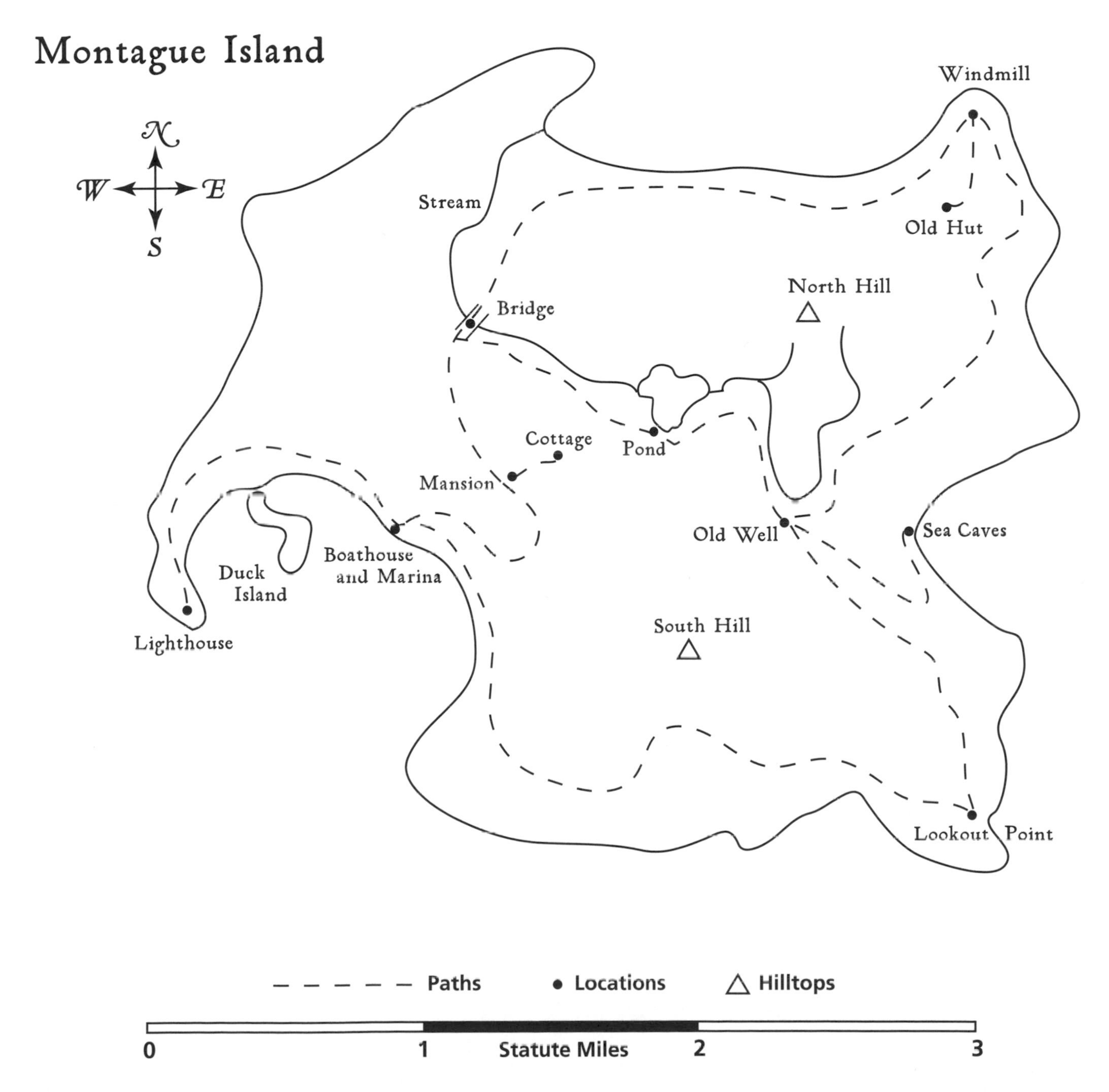

Multi-Chess Tournament

Saturday afternoon, the hosts announce a tournament in which each guest will play one game against each of the other guests. Three different kinds of games will be played in the tournament. From the small game room on the second floor, Alistair brings down a chess set, a shogi set, and a xiangqi set. Shogi and xiangqi are chesslike games that are very popular, and played professionally, in Japan and China, respectively.

The guests are given half an hour to familiarize themselves with the game rules, if necessary, and then pairings are announced for all seven rounds. Each round will consist of three games—one of each type of game. One player (a different one each time) will sit out each round. After seven rounds, each guest will have played one game with every other guest, and each guest will have played two games of chess, two games of shogi, and two games of xiangqi.

The games were played on Saturday night and Sunday. No game ended in a draw. From the following facts, can you determine the order in which the players finished, from most wins to fewest?

1. In one of the rounds, Taylor beat David at chess, Frank beat Charles at shogi, and Jessica beat Beth at xiangqi.
2. In one of the rounds, Karen beat Beth at chess, Frank beat David at shogi, and Taylor beat Charles at xiangqi.
3. When David had a bye, Charles beat Beth at shogi and Taylor beat Karen at xiangqi.
4. The two guests who played chess in the final round were both undefeated in all games in prior rounds.
5. Only one guest lost two chess games.
6. Jessica's shogi record was the same as Karen's xiangqi record, and Karen's shogi record was the same as Jessica's xiangqi record.
7. Two players tied for last place with records of one win and five losses.
8. The winner's two shogi opponents had a better combined record in shogi than the runner-up's shogi opponents did.

○ Beth vs. ○ Charles
○ chess
○ shogi
○ xiangqi

○ Beth vs. ○ David
○ chess
○ shogi
○ xiangqi

○ Beth vs. ○ Frank
○ chess
○ shogi
○ xiangqi

○ Beth vs. ○ Jessica
○ chess
○ shogi
○ xiangqi

○ Beth vs. ○ Karen
○ chess
○ shogi
○ xiangqi

○ Beth vs. ○ Taylor
○ chess
○ shogi
○ xiangqi

○ Charles vs. ○ David
○ chess
○ shogi
○ xiangqi

○ Charles vs. ○ Frank
○ chess
○ shogi
○ xiangqi

○ Charles vs. ○ Jessica
○ chess
○ shogi
○ xiangqi

○ Charles vs. ○ Karen
○ chess
○ shogi
○ xiangqi

○ Charles vs. ○ Taylor
○ chess
○ shogi
○ xiangqi

○ David vs. ○ Frank
○ chess
○ shogi
○ xiangqi

○ David vs. ○ Jessica
○ chess
○ shogi
○ xiangqi

○ David vs. ○ Karen
○ chess
○ shogi
○ xiangqi

○ David vs. ○ Taylor
○ chess
○ shogi
○ xiangqi

○ Frank vs. ○ Jessica
○ chess
○ shogi
○ xiangqi

○ Frank vs. ○ Karen
○ chess
○ shogi
○ xiangqi

○ Frank vs. ○ Taylor
○ chess
○ shogi
○ xiangqi

○ Jessica vs. ○ Karen
○ chess
○ shogi
○ xiangqi

○ Jessica vs. ○ Taylor
○ chess
○ shogi
○ xiangqi

○ Karen vs. ○ Taylor
○ chess
○ shogi
○ xiangqi

On Friday evening of the fourth weekend get-together, the Montagues distribute copies of a floor plan of the mansion and present a small puzzle.

Staff Quarters

The six full-time staff members of the Montague household—head of staff Alistair, chef Evelyn, gardener Grant, nurse Lyle, secretary Molly, and housekeeper Sandy—each live in a different one of the seven staff rooms, labeled S1 through S7 in the floor plan. One of the rooms is unoccupied. From the floor plan shown on the next page and the following clues, can you determine which staffer lives in which room?

1. Alistair and Evelyn are on different floors.
2. Grant and Lyle are on the same floor, and their closets adjoin.
3. Sandy's room is either directly above or directly below Lyle's room.
4. Molly's room's closet is adjacent to the closet of the unoccupied staff room.
5. The sum of Alistair's and Sandy's room numbers is equal to the sum of Evelyn's and Molly's room numbers.

	S1	S2	S3	S4	S5	S6	S7
Alistair							
Evelyn							
Grant							
Lyle							
Molly							
Sandy							
Vacant							

Montague Mansion

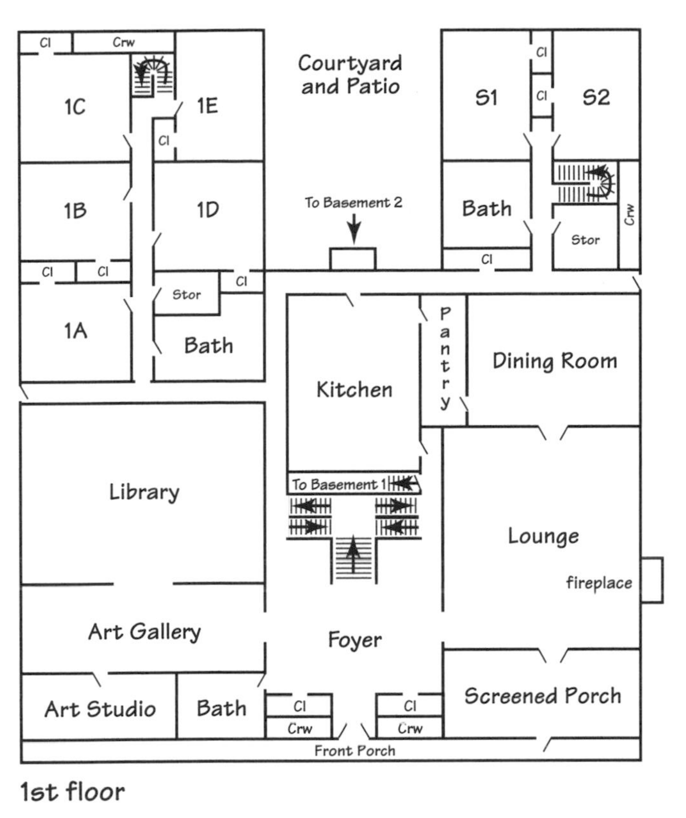

1st floor

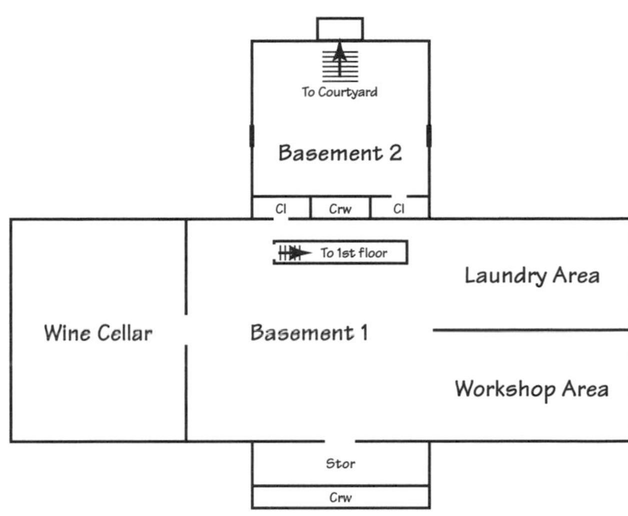

Basements

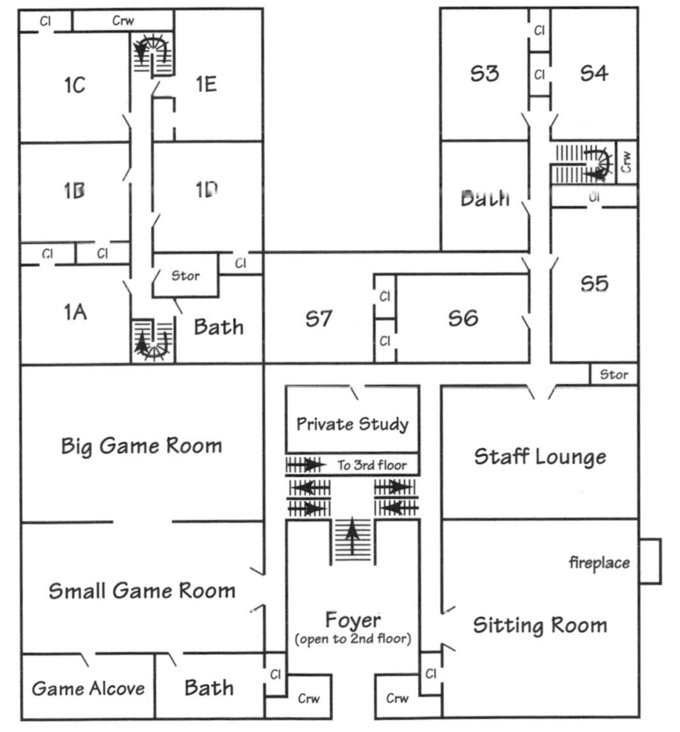

2nd floor

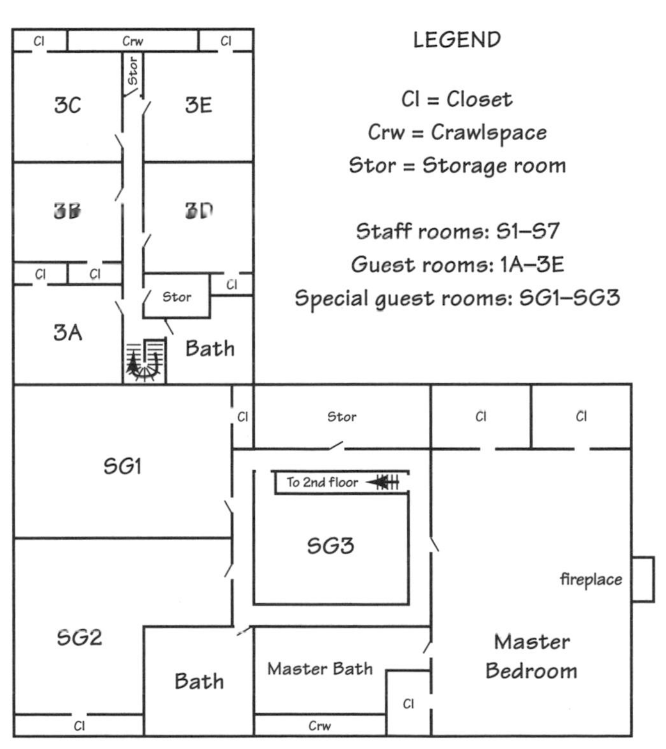

3rd floor

LEGEND

Cl = Closet
Crw = Crawlspace
Stor = Storage room

Staff rooms: S1–S7
Guest rooms: 1A–3E
Special guest rooms: SG1–SG3

Cottage Visitors

The third weekend in May was the first of twelve Montague Island puzzle weekends that would be held on alternate weekends running into the middle of October. The seven guests generally arrive on the Friday before each puzzle weekend and leave on Sunday, then return twelve days later for the next puzzle weekend. However, each of the seven guests was invited to choose one of the twelve-day periods between puzzle weekends to stay in the cottage near the mansion, thereby saving one round trip off and back onto the island. Each guest accepted the invitation and chose a twelve-day period different from any of the other guests' choices, and a schedule was drawn up and posted.

In another of the twelve-day periods, the cottage was scheduled to be occupied by Nolan, the pilot of the Montagues' cabin cruiser and private plane. During the other three twelve-day periods between puzzle weekends, the cottage was scheduled to be unoccupied.

From the clues below, can you determine the order in which Beth, Charles, David, Frank, Jessica, Karen, Taylor, and Nolan were scheduled to occupy the cottage during the eleven periods between puzzle weekends?

1. According to the schedule, the cottage would never be unoccupied in two consecutive periods, nor would it be unoccupied in either the first or last period.
2. Beth was scheduled to stay in the cottage immediately after Karen and immediately before Jessica.
3. Frank was scheduled to stay in the cottage immediately after David and immediately before Taylor.
4. Charles was scheduled to stay in the cottage later in the year than Frank but earlier than Nolan.
5. The first period in which the cottage was unoccupied was the period just before Karen's stay.

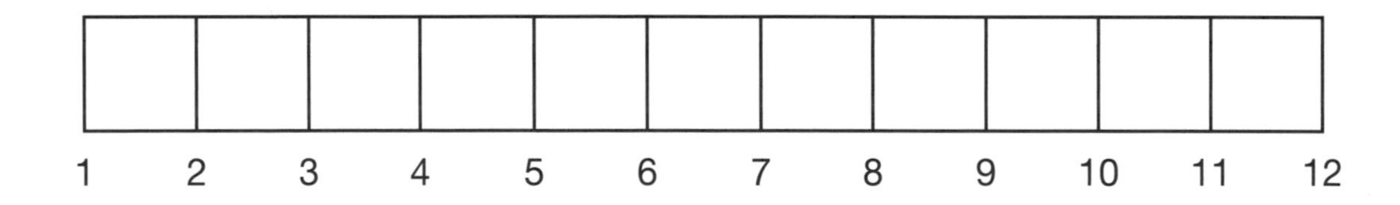

Poisoned

Saturday morning before breakfast, you receive the following note in an envelope.

> **MYSTERY PUZZLE**
>
> **Instructions for Taylor**
>
> Gordon Montague died last night, a few hours after being poisoned during the dinner hour. (Of course, the murder is just part of a game.)
>
> **Required for a complete solution**
>
> Name the guests who committed the crime.
>
> **Statement you are to give to other players**
>
> *The last two guests to leave the dining room included at least one of Beth, Frank, or Karen.*

Statements by the surviving Montague and the staff:

1. Nina Montague: Gordon's glass of wine was poisoned. There were two killers: one guest who poisoned the glass just before dinner, and one guest who removed the evidence right after dinner. The statements they make may be false. Five of the guests are innocent, and their statements are all true.
2. Alistair: We were able to reconstruct the crime after finding the discarded wine glass. We don't know the motive, but Gordon made many enemies over the years while building his fortune.
3. Evelyn: The first guest to enter the dining room after 7 P.M. last night is guilty.
4. Grant: The last guest to leave the dining room before 8 P.M. last night is guilty.
5. Lyle: None of the guests were in the dining room before 7 P.M. or after 8 P.M.
6. Molly: Neither David nor Frank was one of the first two guests to enter the dining room.
7. Sandy: Neither Charles nor Jessica was one of the last two guests to leave the dining room.

Statements by the guests:

8. Beth: Either Jessica was the first person to enter the dining room or David was the last guest to leave, or both.
9. Charles: The first two guests to enter the dining room did not include Charles, Karen, or Taylor; the last two guests to leave the dining room did not include Beth, Frank, or Karen.
10. David: I was not the last guest to leave the dining room; and the first two guests to enter the dining room did not include Charles, Karen, or Taylor.
11. Frank: Either David left the dining room before Charles did or Jessica was not the first person to enter the dining room, or both.
12. Jessica: David was not the last guest to leave the dining room; and the last two guests to leave the dining room did not include Beth, Frank, or Karen.
13. Karen: Either Charles left the dining room before David did or Jessica was not the first person to enter the dining room, or both.
14. Taylor: The last two guests to leave the dining room included at least one of Beth, Frank, or Karen.

Garden Plots

In the spring, a square portion of the vegetable garden was unevenly divided into 14 plots (A–N) for personal use by the seven guests (Beth, Charles, David, Frank, Jessica, Karen, and Taylor) during the growing season, as shown in the diagram below. Each guest chose two plots and planted a different type of vegetable in each plot. The guests weed and water their plots whenever they are on the island, and the Montagues' gardener takes care of the plants when the guests are away.

The vegetables the guests planted were asparagus, broccoli, cabbage, carrots, cucumbers, green beans, lettuce, peas, peppers, potatoes, radishes, squash, tomatoes, and turnips. No two guests selected the same vegetable. From the following clues, can you determine which guest is growing which vegetable in each plot?

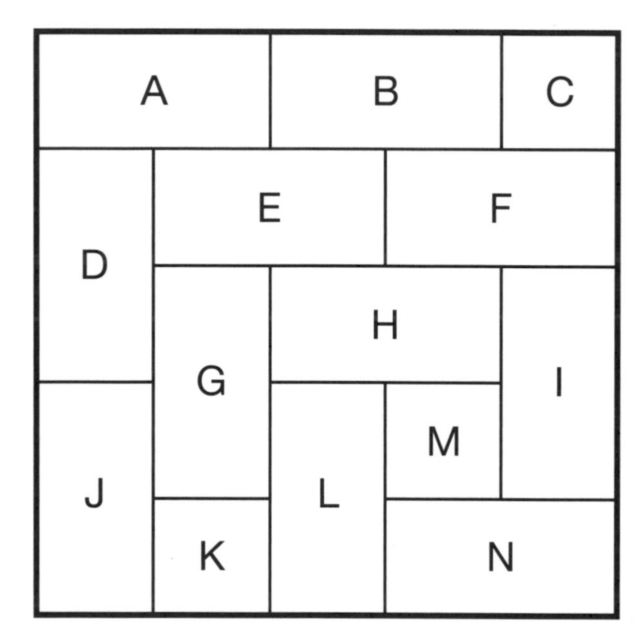

1. Each guest uses two plots that border one another.
2. Plot E borders both of Taylor's plots and one plot each used by Frank, Karen, Jessica, and Charles.
3. Plot G borders both of David's plots and one plot each used by Beth, Charles, Frank, and Taylor.
4. Plot H borders both of Jessica's plots and one plot each used by Beth, Charles, Frank, and Taylor.
5. The four corner plots contain broccoli, carrots, green beans, and radishes.
6. The plots containing asparagus and lettuce both border the plots containing squash and tomatoes, and all four of these vegetables are in plots used by different guests.
7. The plots containing asparagus and peas both border the plots containing cucumbers and turnips, and all four of these vegetables are in plots used by different guests.
8. The plots containing asparagus and squash both border the plots containing tomatoes and turnips, and all four of these vegetables are in plots used by different guests.

9. The plots containing asparagus and turnips both border the plots containing cucumbers and squash, and all four of these vegetables are in plots used by different guests.

10. The plot containing peppers borders the plots containing green beans and potatoes but does not border a plot used by Frank.

11. One of Jessica's plots borders the plots containing potatoes and radishes.

12. David's plots do not contain broccoli or lettuce, nor do they border plots containing either squash or tomatoes.

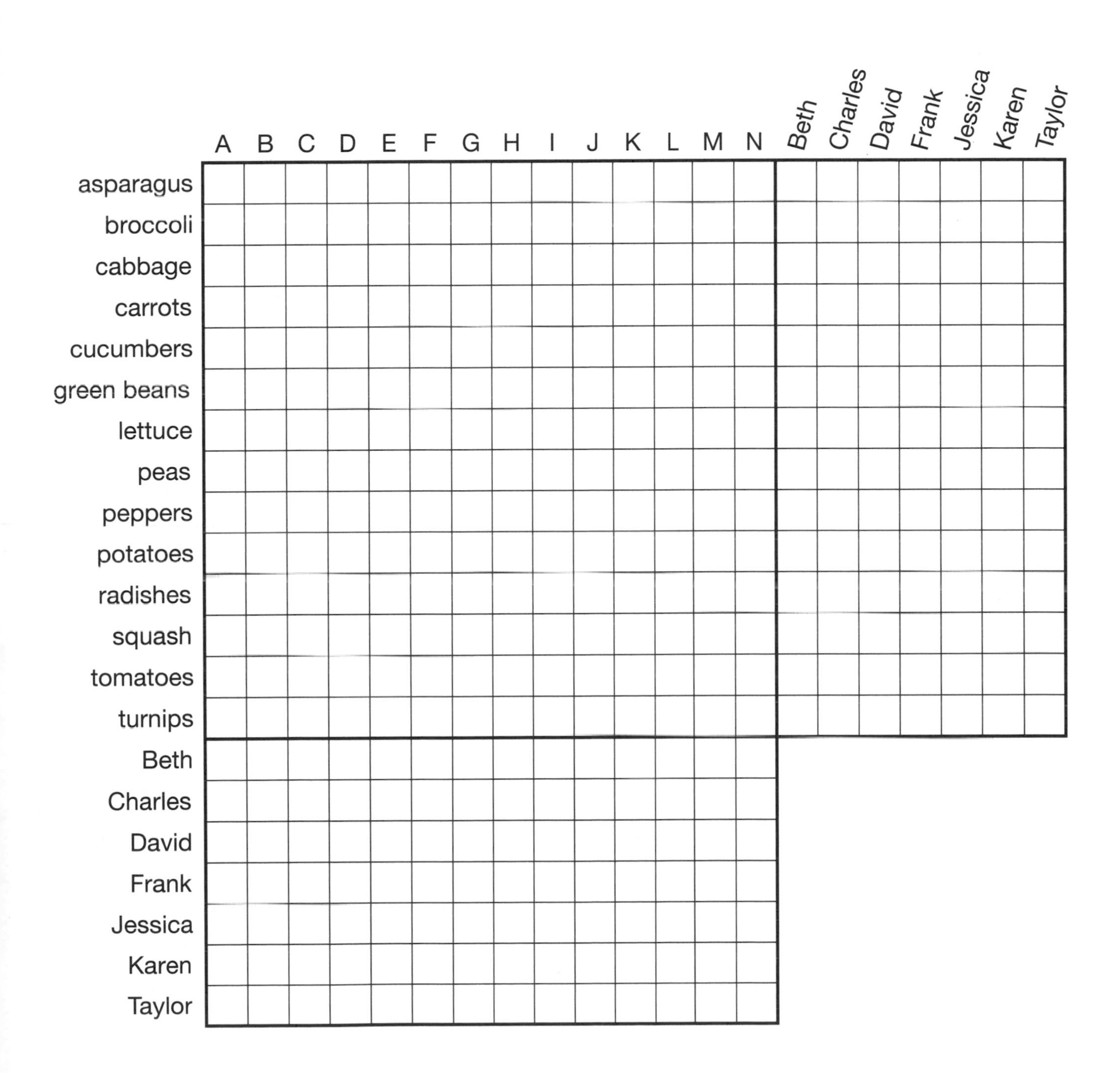

"Have you learned anything yet?" asks Gordon Montague, sitting across from you at a table in a mainland coffee shop.

"So far I only have a working theory," you reply. "But I do have a question: What's behind the two locked doors in the smaller basement?"

"Two doors? Oh, I had forgotten about them. The previous owner—the bank that had foreclosed on the property—didn't have a key to those doors when I bought the island in 2010. We didn't start living here full-time until two years ago, and I never got around to having a locksmith open them. Should I do that?"

"Not just yet, but I'd like to find out as much about the house and the island as possible. Do you know who owned it before the bank?"

"I know the basic history. A family bought the island just after the Civil War and kept it for several generations. They built the mansion around 1870, along with a smaller house that was next to the windmill. Hurricane Hazel destroyed the smaller house in 1954, but the mansion remained intact. The family sold the property in 1973 to a man named Terence Plumly. He and his family lived in the mansion for about 30 years. They made a lot of renovations, such as modernizing the plumbing and heating systems. But both his business and his health began to fail, and he eventually lost the property. I'm not sure what happened to him afterward. We had been keeping an eye out for an island home like this to retire to, so when we learned it was available, Nina contacted the bank and negotiated a price."

"Has anything gone missing since the guests came back this year?"

"Not that I've noticed, but it's hard to keep track of everything we've collected over the years—art, antiques, rare coins, and such. But as I told you when I hired you last fall, it wasn't until late September that I discovered that some of the most valuable postage stamps in our collection, including several recently acquired 1892 Columbian Exposition plate blocks that were worth more than $100,000, had been replaced with forgeries. If I hadn't decided to have the collection reappraised for insurance purposes when I did, it might have been years before I noticed. I know for a fact that the real stamps were in the collection one week and gone the next—and the guests were here during the weekend in between."

You think back to your first meeting with Gordon Montague, when you asked him how well he knew the guests and how they had been chosen. He explained that he had not known any of them personally before last year, but they were all people who, like himself and his wife, serve on boards of multiple charitable foundations. Invitations had gone out to several dozen such people, but only six had accepted. All six are puzzle and game enthusiasts who are single, independently wealthy, and available to travel to the island every other weekend from late spring to early fall. You recommended that the Montagues invite the same six guests back this year, along with you, and all of them had accepted. You also asked Gordon and Nina not to let anyone else know that the stamp forgeries had been discovered.

"I've been checking into the backgrounds of your guests as well as your employees, and also reviewing the security camera footage of the house's entrances," you conclude. "So far I haven't seen anything suspicious. If something new disappears, let me know right away. Otherwise, let's meet here again in eight weeks."

A Hand of Poker

On the fifth puzzle weekend on the island, the seven guests spend Friday evening playing Texas hold 'em, the popular form of poker in which each player is initially dealt two cards face down. After a round of betting, three cards are turned face up ("the flop"), followed by another round of betting. Another card is turned face up ("the turn"), followed by another round of betting, and one final card is turned face up ("the river"), followed by a final round of betting. The five face-up cards are shared by all players, and each player's hand consists of the best five-card poker hand that can be made from their original two cards and the five face-up cards. One hand was turned into a puzzle by the hosts. Players were dealt the following two-card hands:

Beth: ♥Q ♠Q
Charles: ♠6 ♣K
David: ♣A ♣2
Frank: ♣8 ♥5
Jessica: ♠4 ♠7
Karen: ♣5 ♣3
Taylor: ♦6 ♥6

After the flop, which contained no red cards, the players' hands ranked as follows, from best to worst: Taylor, Charles, Beth, Jessica, David, Frank, Karen. After the turn, which was not a diamond, the hands ranked as follows: Taylor, Jessica, Charles, Beth, David, Frank, Karen. After the river, the hands ranked as follows: Karen, Jessica, Taylor, David, Frank, Charles, Beth.

What cards made up the flop, the turn, and the river?

Ranks of Poker Hands

Poker hands rank as follows, from highest to lowest:

straight flush: five cards of the same suit in sequence, such as ♠Q ♠J ♠10 ♠9 ♠8

four of a kind: four cards of the same rank, such as ♠Q ♥Q ♦Q ♣Q, plus any fifth card

full house: three cards of the same rank and a pair of cards of another rank, such as ♠Q ♥Q ♦Q ♠7 ♦7

flush: five cards of the same suit, such as ♠Q ♠10 ♠8 ♠7 ♠2

straight: five cards in sequence, not all of the same suit, such as ♠10 ♥9 ♣8 ♣7 ♦6

three of a kind: three cards of the same rank, plus two other cards

two pair: two cards of the same rank, and two other cards that match in rank

pair: one pair of cards of the same rank

nothing: none of the above

A full house containing the higher-ranking three of a kind beats a full house with a lower-ranking three of a kind. Between hands with two pair, the highest-ranking pair wins; if the hands have the same highest pair, then the other pair is compared. (With four of a kind, three of a kind, or a pair, the highest-ranking set wins.)

Between two flushes, the hand containing the highest card wins; if there is a tie for high card, the second-highest cards are compared, and so on.

Aces may be either high or low in a straight or straight flush. Higher-ranking straights beat lower-ranking straights.

The Lost Goban

Saturday morning you find an envelope that was slipped under your door during the night. It contains this piece of paper:

> **MYSTERY PUZZLE**
>
> **Instructions for Taylor**
>
> A valuable go set, with a kaya wood goban (go board) autographed by a legendary professional go player from Japan, as well as antique Yunzi go stones in mulberry bowls, has disappeared from the mansion. The theft could have taken place weeks ago but was only noticed yesterday. It is feared that the set may have been taken out of the country and sold to an unscrupulous collector.
>
> **Required for a complete solution**
>
> Identify the thief, and also match all the guests to their occupations and the cities they visited.
>
> **Statement you are to give to other players**
>
> *Beth went to either Tokyo or Abu Dhabi.*

In this game, the guests (Beth, Charles, David, Frank, Jessica, Karen, and Taylor) are kept in the dark about their characters' occupations and what foreign city they have recently visited. As usual, the statement by a guest who is a guilty party is not necessarily true, but all other statements can be trusted.

Statements by the Montagues:

1. Gordon: The seven guests' occupations are: historian, investigator, journalist, knitter, linguist, magician, and numismatist. The thief acted alone.
2. Nina: Each guest has recently traveled to one of the following foreign cities: Abu Dhabi, Beijing, Chennai, Manila, Seoul, Singapore, and Tokyo. Two guests took their trips three weeks ago, three took their trips two weeks ago, and two took their trips one week ago. No two guests traveled to the same city.

Statements by the staff:

3. Alistair: Charles, Frank, and Karen are, in some order, the linguist, the magician, and the numismatist. All of them took their trips the same week.
4. Evelyn: Chennai was not visited by the knitter.
5. Grant: Neither the magician nor the numismatist traveled to Beijing.
6. Lyle: Manila was visited by the knitter, the linguist, or the magician. The investigator did not travel to Seoul, but did travel the same week as the thief.

7. Molly: Beth's trip took place in an earlier week than the knitter's, and Jessica traveled in an earlier week than the historian.
8. Sandy: The trips to Chennai and Tokyo were taken the same week.

Statements by the guests:

9. Beth: Charles went to either Abu Dhabi or Beijing.
10. Charles: David went to either Beijing or Chennai.
11. David: Frank went to either Chennai or Manila.
12. Frank: Jessica went to either Manila or Seoul.
13. Jessica: Karen went to either Seoul or Singapore.
14. Karen: Taylor went to either Singapore or Tokyo.
15. Taylor: Beth went to either Tokyo or Abu Dhabi.

	historian	investigator	journalist	knitter	linguist	magician	numismatist	Abu Dhabi	Beijing	Chennai	Manila	Seoul	Singapore	Tokyo
Beth														
Charles														
David														
Frank														
Jessica														
Karen														
Taylor														
Abu Dhabi														
Beijing														
Chennai														
Manila														
Seoul														
Singapore														
Tokyo														

A Relaxing Brunch

On Sunday morning, Evelyn the chef, with considerable help from the Montagues themselves, prepared a remarkable variety of foods for the seven guests (Beth, Charles, David, Frank, Jessica, Karen, and Taylor). Each guest chose one item from each of five categories: one of four kinds of juice (grapefruit, orange, prune, tomato), one of four kinds of omelet (green chili and cheese, jalapeño, mushroom and herb, seafood), one of four kinds of pancake (blueberry, buttermilk, chocolate chip, pecan), one of two kinds of bread (English muffin, wheat toast), and one of four kinds of jelly or jam (boysenberry, grape, red raspberry, strawberry). From the following clues, can you determine who ate and drank which foods?

1. Each of the 18 available food items was chosen by at least one guest, but no food item was chosen by more than four guests.
2. Of the four guests who used strawberry jelly, none of whom was Jessica, no two had the same kind of juice or the same kind of omelet.
3. The three guests who had orange juice all had different kinds of pancakes, none of which was blueberry.
4. The three guests who had seafood omelets used three kinds of jam or jelly, including boysenberry and grape, and two of the three had wheat toast.
5. The one guest who had the jalapeño omelet had an English muffin, while the one guest who had the mushroom and herb omelet had wheat toast.
6. Beth and Taylor both had tomato juice, English muffins, and the same kind of omelets.
7. The guest who drank prune juice did not have a seafood omelet.
8. Jessica and the guest with boysenberry jam had the same kind of omelet.
9. One guest chose both blueberry pancakes and red raspberry jam.
10. Frank and the guest who drank grapefruit juice both had buttermilk pancakes.
11. Charles and the guest who used grape jelly both had pecan pancakes.
12. The two guests who ate chocolate chip pancakes and the two who ate pecan pancakes had four different kinds of omelets.
13. David and Jessica both had English muffins but matched in only one other category, which was not pancakes.
14. Beth and Charles had matching food items in only one category.

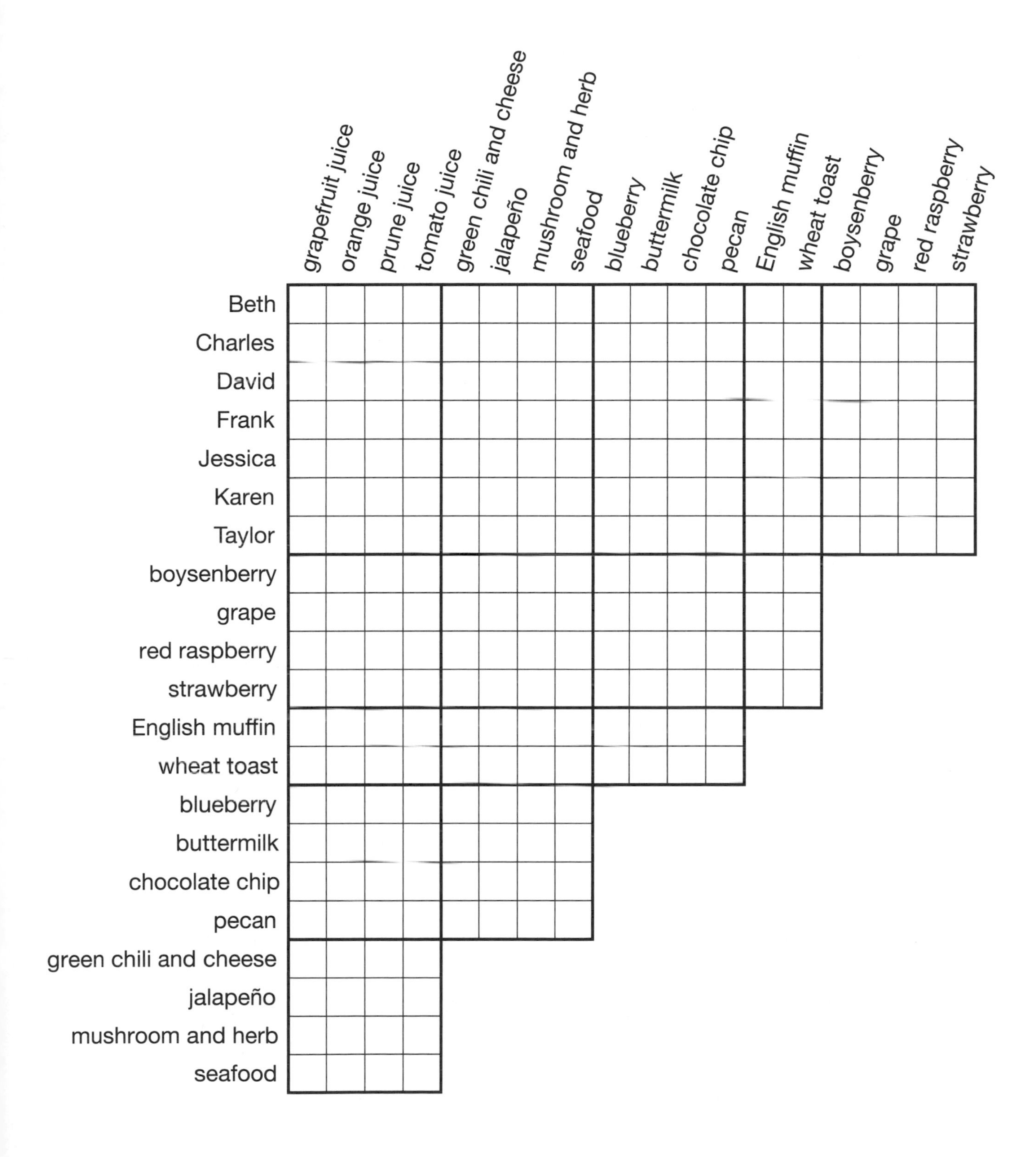
grapefruit juice
orange juice
prune juice
tomato juice
green chili and cheese
jalapeño
mushroom and herb
seafood
blueberry
buttermilk
chocolate chip
pecan
English muffin
wheat toast
boysenberry
grape
red raspberry
strawberry
Beth
Charles
David
Frank
Jessica
Karen
Taylor
boysenberry
grape
red raspberry
strawberry
English muffin
wheat toast
blueberry
buttermilk
chocolate chip
pecan
green chili and cheese
jalapeño
mushroom and herb
seafood

Kidnapped, Part One

During the sixth puzzle weekend, late Saturday morning you receive an envelope containing this piece of paper:

> **MYSTERY PUZZLE**
>
> **Instructions for Taylor**
>
> Nina Montague disappeared while on a walk this morning, and a ransom note has been found.
>
> **Required for a complete solution**
>
> Name the guests involved in the kidnapping.
>
> **Statement you are to give to other players**
>
> *Jessica, Karen, and I were in the dining room this morning between 7 and 7:30. All three of us overheard Gordon Montague tell his wife that he had some work he wanted to do at the cottage right after breakfast. Nina replied that she would take a short walk by herself to the pond and back. I didn't mention any of this to anyone else.*

By late Saturday afternoon you interview everyone and compile the following list of statements:

Statement by Gordon Montague:

1. Gordon: Nina and I didn't take our usual 7:30 A.M. walk together because I had some work to do in the cottage. When I finished at 9:30 and Nina hadn't returned yet, I found out from some of the guests that she had been asked to meet me at the boathouse. I went there straightaway and found a ransom note inside, asking me to transfer $5 million into a certain offshore account if I ever want to see Nina again.

Statements by the staff:

2. Alistair: Two guests are involved in the kidnapping, as well as at least two accomplices from off the island, one of whom must have dropped the other off here by boat a day or two ago. That person then waited for a chance to find Nina alone at the boathouse, and we believe is now holding Nina captive somewhere on the island.
3. Evelyn: One, and only one, of the guests who overheard Gordon and Nina's plans for the morning is guilty.
4. Grant: At least one of the following guests is guilty: Beth, Charles, Jessica, Karen.
5. Lyle: At least one of the following guests is guilty: Charles, Frank, Karen, Taylor.
6. Molly: At least one of the following guests is guilty: Beth, Frank, Karen, Taylor. If Karen is guilty, then David is innocent.
7. Sandy: If Beth is guilty, then Karen and Taylor are innocent. If Charles is guilty, then Taylor is innocent. And if Karen is guilty, then both Frank and Charles are innocent.

Statements by the guests:

8. Beth: I told two of the other guests that if they see Nina, they should ask her to meet Gordon at the boathouse, because that is what I had heard from another guest.

9. Charles: I told two of the other guests that if they see Nina, they should ask her to meet Gordon at the boathouse, because that is what I had heard from another guest.

10. David: I saw Nina walking back from the direction of the bridge and told her that Gordon wanted her to meet him at the boathouse, because that is what I had heard from another guest.

11. Frank: I told two of the other guests that if they see Nina, they should ask her to meet Gordon at the boathouse, because that is what I had heard from another guest.

12. Jessica: Karen, Taylor, and I were in the dining room this morning between 7 and 7:30. All three of us overheard Gordon Montague tell his wife that he had some work he wanted to do at the cottage right after breakfast. Nina replied that she would take a short walk by herself to the pond and back. I didn't mention any of this to anyone else.

13. Karen: Jessica, Taylor, and I were in the dining room this morning between 7 and 7:30. All three of us overheard Gordon Montague tell his wife that he had some work he wanted to do at the cottage right after breakfast. Nina replied that she would take a short walk by herself to the pond and back. I didn't mention any of this to anyone else.

14. Taylor: Jessica, Karen, and I were in the dining room this morning between 7 and 7:30. All three of us overheard Gordon Montague tell his wife that he had some work he wanted to do at the cottage right after breakfast. Nina replied that she would take a short walk by herself to the pond and back. I didn't mention any of this to anyone else.

(As for where Nina is being held captive, see the next puzzle.)

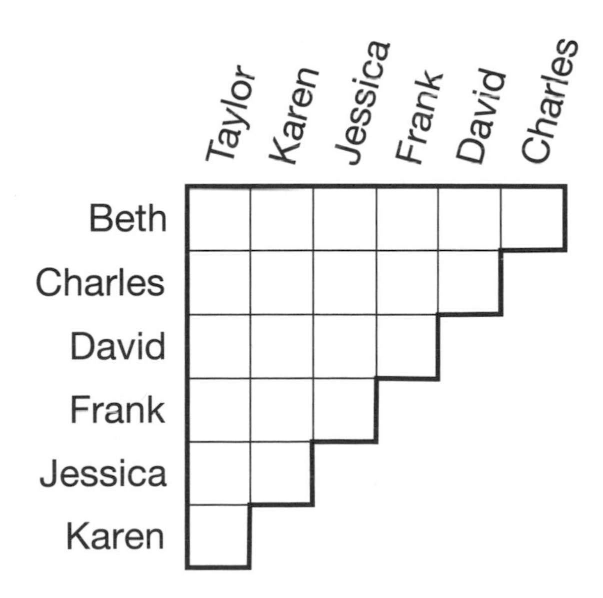

Kidnapped, Part Two

After she was kidnapped, Nina was held captive at one of the seven locations marked A through G on the map of the island. If exactly four of the following statements are true but the other one is false, where is the location?

1. The location is either farther north than the bridge or farther west than the pond, but not both.
2. The location is either farther east than the sea caves or farther west than the bridge.
3. The location is either farther east than North Hill or farther north than South Hill, but not both.
4. The location is either closer (as the crow flies) to the lighthouse than to the windmill or farther south than North Hill, but not both.
5. The location is either farther west than the mansion or farther north than the pond, but not both.

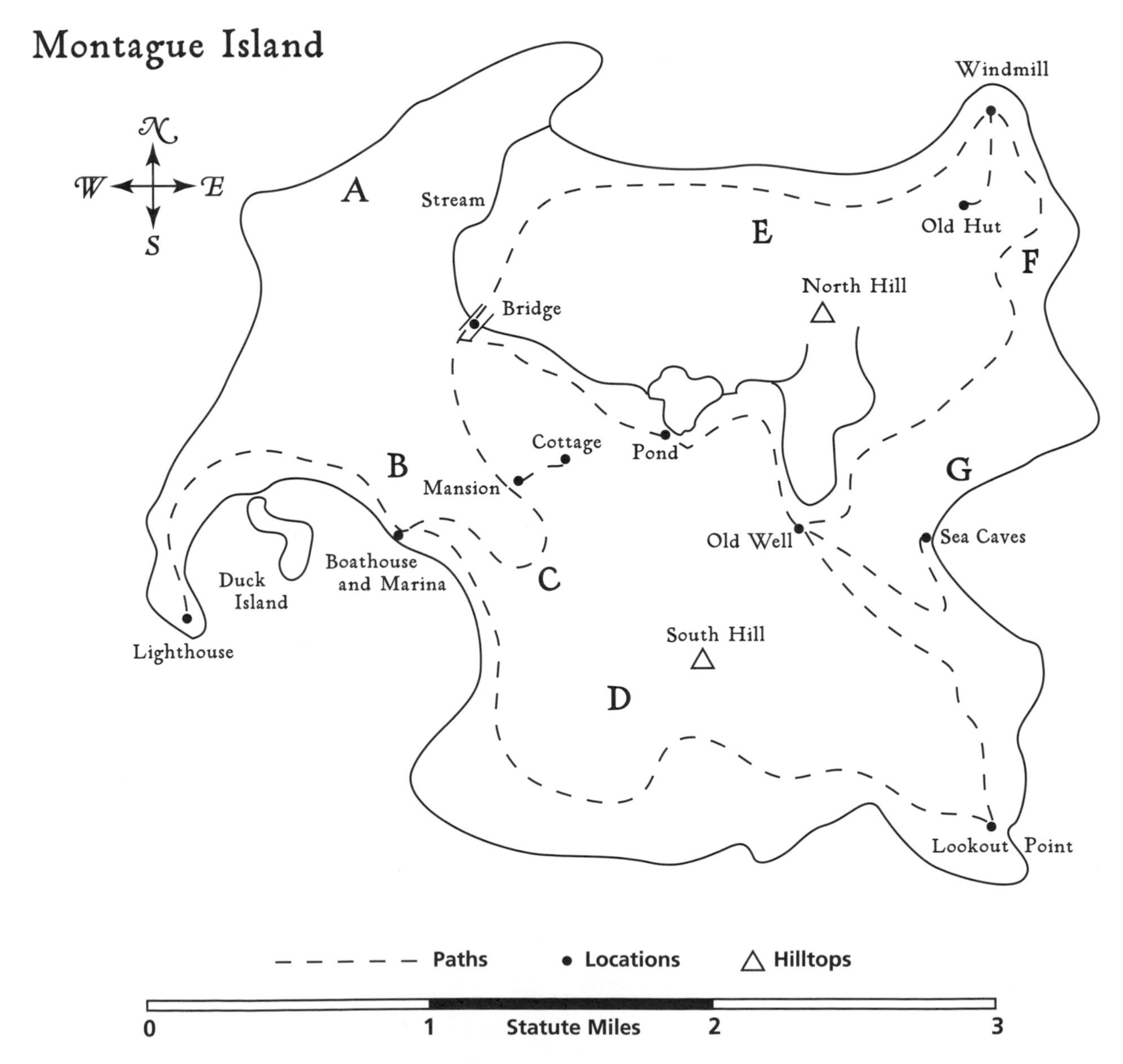

A Cribbage Tournament

Nolan, the Montagues' pilot, lives on the mainland but often stays in the cabin on weekends. He is a card game enthusiast, and on Sunday he joins the seven guests (Beth, Charles, David, Frank, Karen, Jessica, and Taylor) to participate in a one-day cribbage tournament. The eight players are randomly assigned to either Group 1 or Group 2, each of which consists of four players. Each group then holds its own double round-robin tournament—that is, each player in the group plays two games against each of the other three, making a total of six games played by each player.

After the double round-robins, the semifinals consist of the winner of Group 1 playing the runner-up in Group 2, while the winner of Group 2 plays the runner-up in Group 1. This way, if the two best players happen to have been placed in the same group, they can still meet in the finals.

From the following clues, can you determine which players were in which group, what their won-lost records were during the double round-robin portion of the tournament, and who won the final match between the winners of the semifinals?

1. Charles and Nolan were the only players with the same won-lost records after the double round-robin portion of the tournament. One of them finished third in Group 1 and the other finished second in Group 2.
2. Frank and Taylor met in one of the semifinals.
3. In the double round-robin portion of the tournament, the number of games won by Jessica was equal to the sum of the number of games won by David and Taylor.
4. Karen, who was in the same group as Nolan, won more games than Beth.
5. In both semifinals as well as the finals, the player who had won fewer games in the double round-robin was victorious.

	Group 1				Group 2			
	1st	2nd	3rd	4th	1st	2nd	3rd	4th
Beth								
Charles								
David								
Frank								
Jessica								
Karen								
Nolan								
Taylor								
WINS								

Murder in the Staff Lounge

The seventh puzzle weekend of the year began with an uneventful Friday night. But Saturday morning, the guests receive envelopes containing instructions as well as two special cards—one indicating a weapon and the other indicating a motive. The cards are to be kept by each player but are not to be shown to the other players.

MYSTERY PUZZLE

Instructions for Taylor

Housekeeper Sandy has been found murdered in the staff lounge on the second floor. All the guests (Beth, Charles, David, Frank, Jessica, Karen, and Taylor) had the opportunity to commit the crime.

Required for a complete solution

Determine the killer, the weapon used, and the motive for the crime.

Statement you are to give to other players

Neither Karen nor the person whose weapon is the stone owl has blackmail for a motive, and Frank's weapon is not the lamp.

Statements by the Montagues:

1. Gordon: The players—the seven guests—have each been given a card depicting one of these murder weapons: bookend, candlestick, lamp, paperweight, stone owl, trivet, vase. They are to keep these cards throughout the game. No two guests have cards showing the same weapon. In the correct solution to the crime, the murder weapon is the one on the card held by the guilty player.
2. Nina: Each player has been given a card showing one of the following possible motives for the crime: anger, blackmail, fear, greed, revenge. Each of these motives has been assigned to at least one guest. In the correct solution to the crime, the motive will be the one on the card held by the guilty player.

Statements by the staff:

3. Alistair: The killer acted alone and is the only guest whose statement may be false.
4. Evelyn: The guests with the lamp, paperweight, and trivet as weapons do not have anger or blackmail as motives. The guests with the bookend and vase as weapons do not have the motives fear or greed. The guests with the candlestick and stone owl as weapons do not have revenge as their motive.
5. Grant: David and Jessica both have revenge as their motive.
6. Lyle: Jessica's weapon is either the bookend, candlestick, stone owl, or vase.
7. Molly: Beth, Karen, and Taylor do not have motives of fear, greed, or revenge.

Statements by the guests:

8. Beth: The person whose weapon is the lamp does not have greed as a motive, nor the same motive as any other player. My weapon is not the stone owl.
9. Charles: My weapon is not the lamp.
10. David: The guest whose weapon is the candlestick does not have anger as a motive, but two other guests do.
11. Frank: My weapon is not the lamp.
12. Jessica: Neither Charles nor Frank has the trivet for his weapon.
13. Karen: One of the guests whose motive is revenge has the bookend for a weapon.
14. Taylor: Neither Karen nor the person whose weapon is the stone owl has blackmail for a motive, and Frank's motive is not fear.

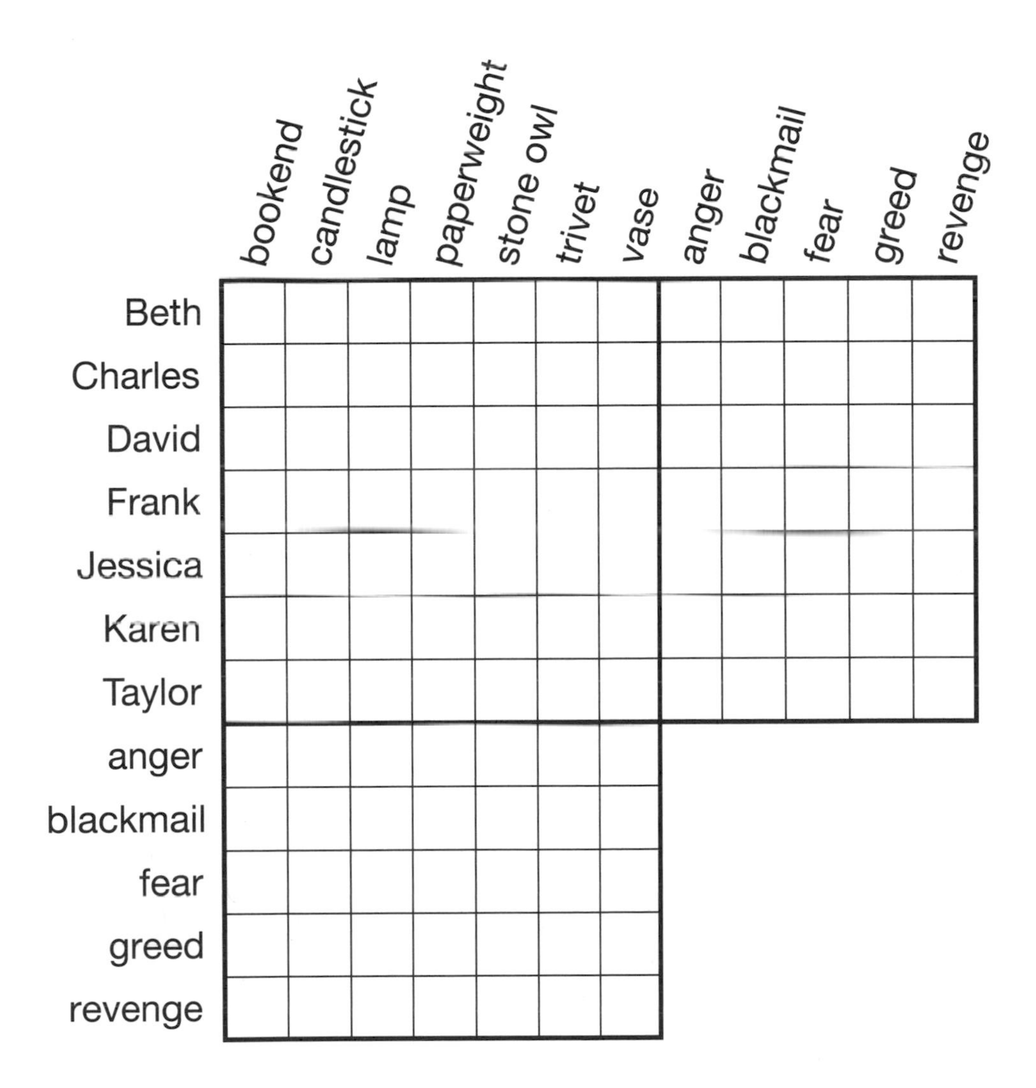

The Mystery Novels

Each of the seven guests (Beth, Charles, David, Frank, Jessica, Karen, and Taylor) is currently reading a different mystery novel from the following group: *Cards on the Chair, Dead Woman's Folly, Dog Among the Pigeons, Elephants Can Forget, Evil Under the Moon, Life on the Nile, Three-Act Comedy.* From the clues below, can you determine which guest is reading which book, as well as the age of each guest? (In these clues, age is measured in whole years based on the guest's most recent birthday.)

1. No two of the guests are the same age, none is younger than 30, and none is older than 60.
2. The fourth-oldest guest is 48 years old.
3. The only two guests who are just one year apart in age are Jessica and Taylor, neither of whom is over 50.
4. The largest age difference between a guest and the next-younger or next-older guest is between Frank and Taylor.
5. The two youngest guests are reading *Elephants Can Forget* and *Three-Act Comedy.*
6. The two oldest guests are reading *Cards on the Chair* and *Life on the Nile.*
7. There are two guests who prefer to read in the lounge, and the age of one of them is exactly two-thirds the age of the other. There are two other guests who prefer to read in the library, and the age of one of them is exactly three-quarters the age of the other. And there are two guests who prefer to read in their rooms, and the age of one of them is exactly four-fifths the age of the other. There are no other instances in which the age of any of the seven guests is exactly two-thirds, three-quarters, or four-fifths the age of any other guest.
8. The age of the one guest who prefers to read in the sitting room (and who is not reading *Dog Among the Pigeons*) becomes the age of one of the other guests when its digits are reversed.
9. Both Beth and Charles are older than Karen, who is older than the person reading *Dog Among the Pigeons.*
10. Taylor is not reading *Three-Act Comedy*, and Karen is not reading *Dead Woman's Folly.*
11. Beth is younger than the guest who is reading *Cards on the Chair.*

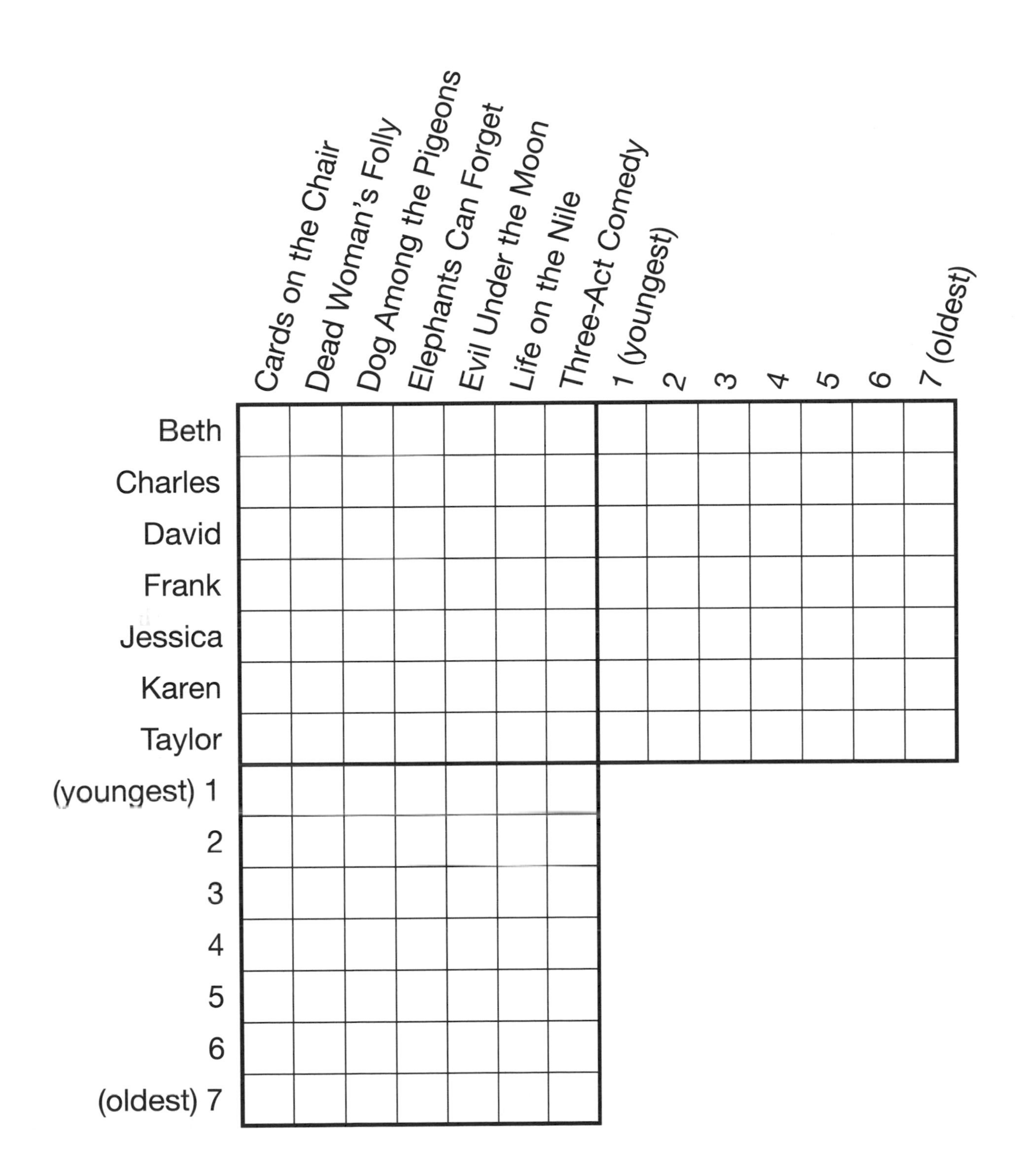

Cards on the Chair
Dead Woman's Folly
Dog Among the Pigeons
Elephants Can Forget
Evil Under the Moon
Life on the Nile
Three-Act Comedy
1 (youngest)
2
3
4
5
6
7 (oldest)
Beth
Charles
David
Frank
Jessica
Karen
Taylor
(youngest) 1
2
3
4
5
6
(oldest) 7

Mug Shots

The guests are in the dining room early Sunday morning, discussing the weekend's earlier events over a hot beverage. Six of the guests are having espresso drinks of various strengths, and the seventh guest is having decaf coffee.

Each guest is drinking from a mug that he or she has been using regularly since the first puzzle weekend. The mugs are from a single set of a dozen mugs, each of which is decorated with two different kinds of geometric shapes—one shape on the top half of the mug, the other on the bottom half. The shapes are diamonds, dots, stars, and triangles. Each of the possible combinations of two of these shapes can be found on two mugs in the full set. When two mugs have the same combination of shapes, the shape that is on top on one mug is on the bottom on the other mug, making it possible to distinguish all 12 mugs from one another.

From the clues below, can you determine which guest is having which drink, and what two shapes decorate each guest's mug?

1. Of the guests not having decaf, two are having one shot of espresso each, two are having two shots each, and the other two are each having three shots.
2. Charles and Taylor are the only two guests whose mug designs use the same pair of shapes.
3. Of the four guests with triangle designs on their mugs, one has one shot, two have two shots, and one has three shots of espresso.
4. The three guests with dots on their cups drink decaf, two shots of espresso, and three shots of espresso.
5. Both Beth and Karen have stars on their mugs.
6. The guests who drink one shot of espresso and the guests who drink three shots all have stars on their mugs.
7. Beth drinks more shots of espresso than Charles and Jessica drinks more shots than Karen.
8. There are no diamonds on David's mug.

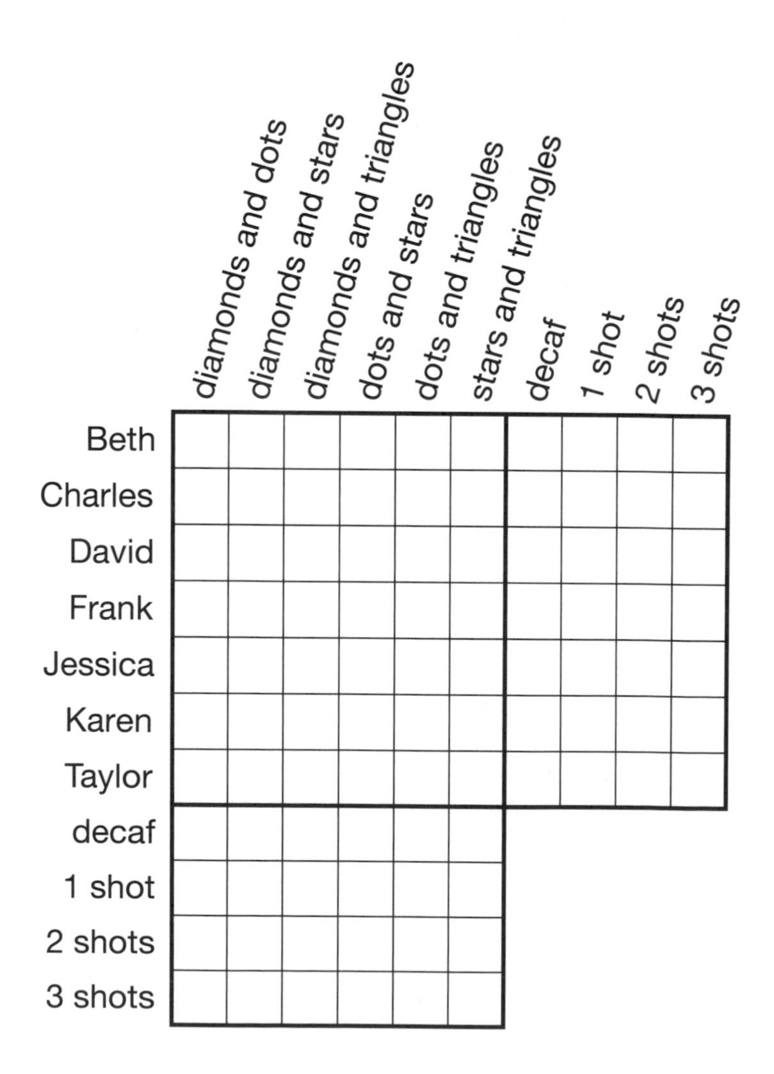

Masquerade

It's Friday night at Montague mansion. Taylor, having been chosen as emcee for a trivia game focusing on costumed superheroes, has divided the other six guests into two teams of three to compete against one another.

For this occasion the six guests have all dressed up as superheroes. The three women—Beth, Karen, and Jessica—have dressed up as Chatwoman, Scarlet Wish, and Stormy, not necessarily in that order. The men—Charles, David, and Frank—have dressed up as Green Sparrow, the Incredible Hunk, and Ironic Man, not necessarily in that order. From the clues below, can you determine who wore each costume and which guests made up each three-person trivia game team?

1. Beth and Jessica are not on the same team.
2. Charles and David are not on the same team.
3. Chatwoman and the Incredible Hunk are not on the same team.
4. Green Sparrow and Scarlet Wish are not on the same team.
5. Beth and Ironic Man are not on the same team.
6. Jessica is not Scarlet Wish.
7. If Beth is Stormy, Karen is on her team.
8. If David is the Incredible Hunk, Frank is on his team.
9. If Frank is Green Sparrow, Jessica is not Chatwoman.
10. If Frank is not Green Sparrow, Beth is not Scarlet Wish.

	Chatwoman	Scarlet Wish	Stormy
Beth			
Karen			
Jessica			

	Green Sparrow	Incredible Hunk	Ironic Man
Charles			
David			
Frank			

TEAM 1

____

____

____

TEAM 2

____

____

____

The Open Safe

Late Saturday afternoon, you receive instructions for the next puzzle.

MYSTERY PUZZLE

Instructions for Taylor

As Molly was putting some documents into the safe in the private study on the second floor at 2 P.M. on Saturday, someone came up behind her, knocked her unconscious, and stole some items from the safe. From the following statements that were made later the same afternoon, can you determine which guest was the thief?

Required for a complete solution

Name the thief, and also determine each guest's occupation and astrological sign.

Statement you are to give to other players

Neither the radiologist nor Karen was in the library around 2 P.M. My sign is not Aquarius.

Statements by the Montagues:

1. Gordon: The thief acted alone. The guests' occupations in this weekend's game are ornithologist, paleontologist, radiologist, seismologist, toxicologist, vulcanologist, and zoologist. All of the guests' statements, including the thief's, are true.
2. Nina: I'm an amateur astrologer, and this week I prepared horoscope charts for each guest based on the times and dates they were born. The guests' astrological signs are Aquarius, Gemini, Libra, Pisces, Scorpio, Taurus, and Virgo.

Statements by the staff:

3. Alistair: Just before 2 P.M., Taylor, whose sign is not Pisces, was outdoors; the library and the sitting room were occupied by the seismologist and the Virgo, not necessarily in that order; two guests were in the lounge; and the big game room and small game room were occupied by one guest each. Of these rooms, only the library and lounge are on the first floor.
4. Evelyn: The astrological signs of the toxicologist, vulcanologist, and zoologist are Aquarius, Pisces, and Scorpio, not necessarily in that order.
5. Grant: Charles and the guests who have the signs Gemini and Taurus were in the two game rooms and the sitting room, in some order, just before 2 P.M.
6. Lyle: The vulcanologist was not in the sitting room around 2 P.M. The paleontologist is innocent.
7. Molly: At 2 P.M. I was in the private study on the second floor, putting some documents in the safe, when someone hit me over the head, knocking me out. A few seconds before, I heard someone coming up the stairs from the first floor, and that must have been the thief.
8. Sandy: Neither the ornithologist nor the Taurus was in the small game room around 2 P.M.

Statements by the guests:

9. Beth: At 2 P.M. today I was in the lounge talking to the guest whose sign is Libra. Neither of us left to go upstairs. My sign is not Aquarius.
10. Charles: Neither the paleontologist nor Jessica has the sign Libra.
11. David: Around 2 P.M. I was not in the library or small game room, but was indoors, as was the zoologist. I am not the vulcanologist.
12. Frank: This morning I played a game of chess with the vulcanologist as Beth and Taylor watched.
13. Jessica: Last night I played bridge with the guests whose signs are Aquarius and Virgo as well as the person who was in the small game room today at 2 P.M.
14. Karen: Earlier today I played tennis matches with the seismologist and vulcanologist.
15. Taylor: Neither the radiologist nor Karen was in the library around 2 P.M. My sign is not Aquarius.

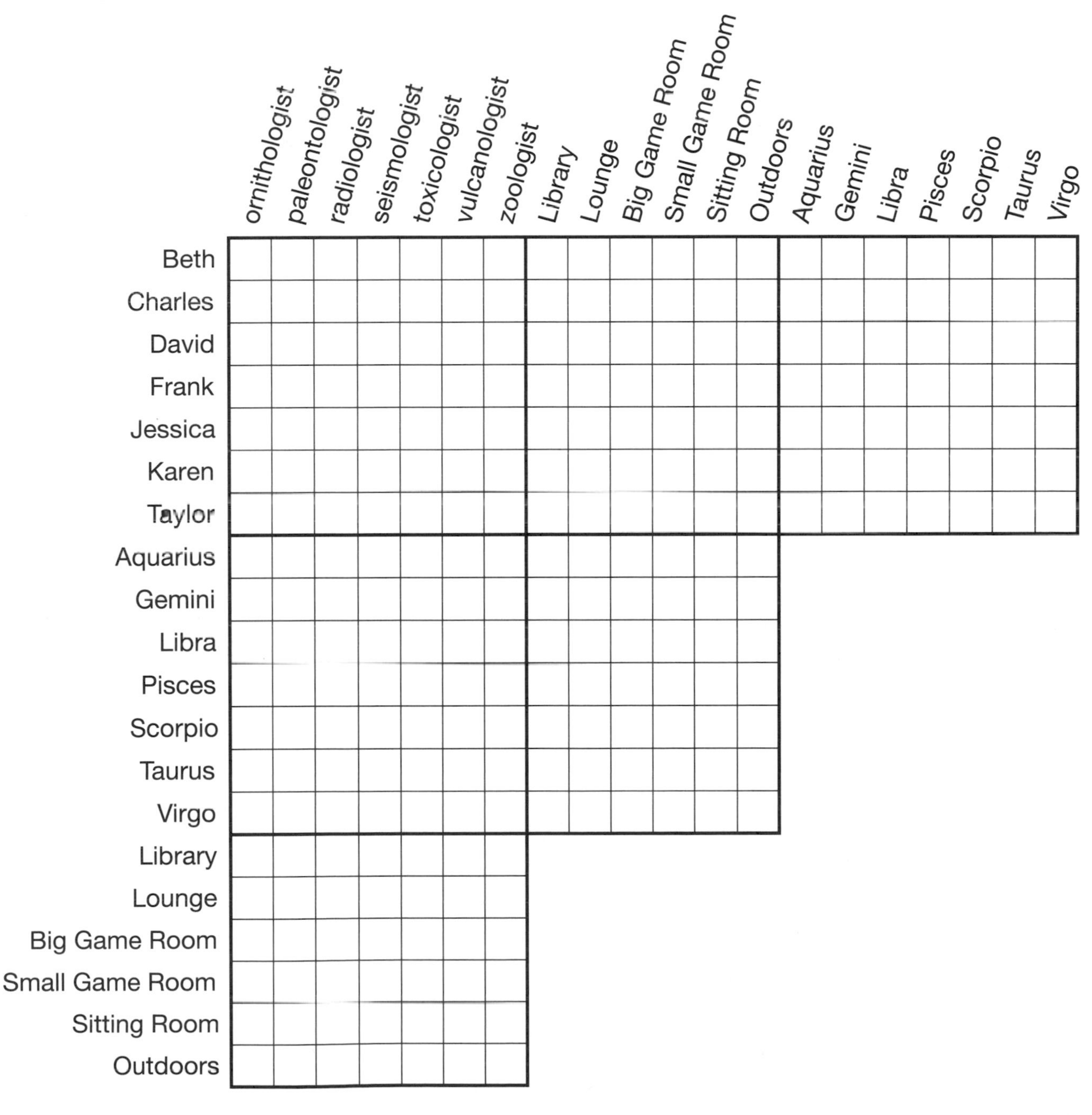

Fifty-Fifty

"Here's a deduction game that may remind you of some other games you've seen," Gordon Montague begins, as the guests are gathered around him in the lounge. "But because it is played with cards, there are two different elements to deduce—the ranks and suits of a set of cards. I have randomly dealt out five cards from a standard 52-card deck face down in a row. You have a supply of as many decks of cards as you need, which you will use to make guesses about what cards are in the row I dealt out.

"Each of you, in turn, will deal five cards face up below my row of cards. I will compare your cards with mine and give a four-digit score to your guess. The first digit indicates how many cards of yours match a card in my row in rank and are in the same position in the rows. The second digit indicates how many cards in your row match one of my cards in rank but are in a different position. In determining the second digit, any cards—both in my row and yours—that matched in rank and position, and so were counted in the first digit, are disregarded. The third number indicates how many cards of yours match the suit of a card in my row in suit and are in the same position. The fourth number tells you how many cards in your row—disregarding any cards in our rows that matched in both suit and position, and so were counted in the third digit—have a suit that matches one of my cards but is not in the same position.

"The goal is to make a series of guesses that end up with my giving you a result of 5050—which is why I call this game Fifty-Fifty. A score of 5050 for a guess means that all five cards in your guess have the correct rank and suit and are in the correct positions.

"Here's an example. Suppose I deal the following cards face down…

♠10 ♥J ♥6 ♣6 ♠Q

…and suppose your first guess is:

♠8 ♦J ♣3 ♣9 ♥A

"This guess will earn a score of 1021: one card matching mine in rank and in the right position (the jack); no cards matching mine in rank in the wrong position; two cards matching mine in suits in the correct positions (the spade in the first position and the club in the fourth position; the club in the correct position takes precedence over the other club); and one card matching mine in suit but in the wrong position (the heart). Note that the heart only scores 1 point even though there are two hearts in my row. To score 2 points for my two hearts, your guess would have to have included two hearts."

Five of the guests venture guesses, each of which is awarded a score by Gordon. After studying the guesses and responses, Jessica announces that she knows all five face-down cards. What are they?

						Score
Face-down:	▯	▯	▯	▯	▯	
Guess #1	♠2	♥3	♦A	♣K	♠Q	0312
Guess #2	♥7	♦8	♣9	♠10	♥J	0113
Guess #3	♦4	♣5	♥6	♥7	♦7	1112
Guess #4	♥Q	♥7	♥K	♣7	♠3	3031
Guess #5	♦7	♥K	♥2	♥7	♠A	3112
Jessica	?	?	?	?	?	5050

"It's finally happened again," Gordon tells you, "and this time it's even more puzzling. We've been keeping the door to our master bedroom locked, and only Nina and I have keys. Yet sometime in the past month, Nina's single most valuable piece of jewelry—a diamond necklace—was replaced with one that looks very similar but has imitation gems. The original was kept in a jewelry case on her dresser."

"I'd like to test a theory," you propose. "Can you subtly make it known to guests and staff that you have acquired a new postage stamp of high value? Maybe an early U.S. commemorative with a misprint, or the famous inverted Jenny airmail stamp? I can't guarantee that the stamp won't get stolen, though I could alert dealers to be on the lookout for it in case someone tries to sell it."

"Yes, I can do that," Gordon replies. "I still keep my stamp albums in a bookcase in the master bedroom, but it seems the thief has figured out a way to gain access."

"I suspect that someone on your staff is involved, likely with the help of one of the guests. I've ruled out Alistair, since he's been with you for 15 years, and I've determined that Nolan is also above suspicion. But the other staff people were all hired after you moved here just two years ago. I've learned that some of them have secrets."

"How will we proceed?"

"Wait until Sunday of the next-to-last puzzle weekend to add the new stamp to your collection and let people know about it. I want to try to give the guests too little time for any of them to steal it themselves without being noticed. None of them will be in the cottage between those weekends—only Nolan will. You will check on the stamp a few times a day, and if the stamp has not yet been stolen, I'll try to keep close tabs on the guests during the final puzzle weekend, perhaps forcing the staff member to steal it."

Gordon looks a bit skeptical but lets you continue.

"I have an idea about how things are being taken without being noticed. If I'm right, I may have a way to identify the thieves if they strike again. But that means continuing to let them think for now that you haven't noticed the replaced necklace, or for that matter the forged stamps."

"All right," Gordon agrees, "people I trust say you're the best at this kind of thing, so I'll do as you say."

You hand Gordon a business card of someone who occasionally works for you. "No one is scheduled to stay at the cottage this week. Arrange for this person to come out and stay there for a few days. Tell anyone who asks that he's an old acquaintance who needs a quiet place to write."

Popularity Contest

"We're going to conduct a small survey," Gordon Montague explained to the seven guests on Friday evening of the ninth puzzle weekend. "We want each of you to rank the other six guests in terms of friendliness. Give a ranking of 6 to the guest you consider the friendliest, 5 to the next most friendly, and so forth, with 1 being the least friendly. You will not be ranking yourselves. Afterward, there will be a little puzzle in which you try to determine all the rankings that everyone gave everyone else. But don't worry about hurting anyone's feelings—in the puzzle I will give you, everyone's names will have been changed to preserve anonymity."

Here is the puzzle Gordon created before changing the guests' names and presenting it to them. From the following clues, can you determine the rankings each guest gave every other guest?

1. Beth, Jessica, and Karen all gave the same ranking to Taylor, which happened to be the same ranking that Beth was given by Frank.
2. Charles, David, and Frank all gave Jessica the same ranking, but they gave three different rankings to Taylor.
3. Beth and Charles gave each other the same ranking, and so did Beth and David, and so did Charles and David.
4. Beth ranked Jessica the same as David ranked Taylor, and she ranked Karen the same as Charles ranked Taylor.
5. Frank gave Charles the same ranking as Beth did.
6. The ranking that Beth gave Frank was the same ranking that two other guests gave Frank and that Taylor gave Beth.
7. Karen was given the same ranking by Frank and Jessica, and it was the same as the rankings given to David by Karen and Taylor.
8. Karen was given the same ranking by David and Taylor, and it was the same as the ranking given to David by Jessica and the ranking Karen gave Beth.
9. Charles was given the same ranking by Karen and Taylor, and it was the same as the rankings given by Jessica to Beth and by Frank to David.
10. The ranking given to Karen by Beth was the same as a ranking that another guest gave Beth.
11. Karen gave Jessica the same ranking as Taylor gave Frank.
12. Three of the rankings that Frank received were the same as three of the rankings that Taylor received.
13. The ranking received by the greatest number of guests was 1, and the ranking received by the second greatest number of guests was 2.
14. The ranking received by the fewest guests was 6, and the ranking received by the second smallest number of guests was 5.
15. Of the two rankings that were received by the same number of guests, the higher number was received by one of the guests three times.

Guests Giving Rankings \ Guests Receiving Rankings	Beth	Charles	David	Frank	Jessica	Karen	Taylor
Beth	X						
Charles		X					
David			X				
Frank				X			
Jessica					X		
Karen						X	
Taylor							X

Murder at the Cottage

After lunch on Saturday, the guests hear that a murder has just been committed on the island.

MYSTERY PUZZLE

Instructions for Taylor

A stranger was murdered at the cottage today sometime between 8 A.M. and noon.

Required for a complete solution

Identify which guest (Beth, Charles, David, Frank, Karen, Jessica, or yourself) is the killer.

Statement you are to give to other players

Either Frank was in the small game room all morning from 8 A.M. to noon, or Karen left that room at 10 A.M., or both.

Statements by the Montagues:

1. Gordon: Nolan, our cabin cruiser pilot, is staying at the cottage this weekend. This morning, he left the cottage at 8 A.M. to do an errand on the mainland. When he returned to the cabin at noon, he found the body of a man in his twenties inside.
2. Nina: The motive was blackmail. One of our guests was supposed to pay the victim to keep silent about a past crime. But instead of cash, the blackmail victim gave him a fatal stab with the sword that is usually on display in our sitting room.

Statements by the staff:

3. Alistair: The killer acted alone, and is the only guest who may make a false statement.
4. Evelyn: The sitting room was empty most of the morning, and so anyone could have taken the sword without being seen.
5. Grant: Nolan left the cottage unlocked, as he usually does when he plans to return the same day.
6. Lyle: I examined the body, and I believe the murder occurred around 11 A.M.
7. Molly: Any guest who spent the whole morning in either the large game room or small game room could not have committed the crime.
8. Sandy: By 12:15 P.M. all the guests were seated at the dining room table, eating lunch.

Statements by the guests:

9. Beth: Charles and David were in the large game room all morning from 8 A.M. to noon. Jessica and Taylor were there too, but left at 10.
10. Charles: Of Beth, Frank, Karen, at least one of them was in the small game room all morning from 8 A.M. to noon.
11. David: Of Beth, Frank, and Karen, at least one of them left the small game room at 10 A.M.
12. Frank: Either Karen was in the small game room all morning from 8 A.M. to noon, or Beth left that room at 10 A.M., or both.
13. Karen: Either Beth was in the small game room all morning from 8 A.M. to noon, or Frank left that room at 10 A.M., or both.
14. Jessica: If Frank is innocent, so is Karen. And if Karen is innocent, so is Frank.
15. Taylor: Either Frank was in the small game room all morning from 8 A.M. to noon, or Karen left that room at 10 A.M., or both.

A Night at the Opera

The guests have decided to spend Saturday evening watching an opera. The Montagues have eight operas in their DVD collection to choose from: *Aida, Carmen, Die Walküre, Il trovatore, Le nozze di Figaro, Les contes d'Hoffman, Rigoletto,* and *Tosca.* Gordon Montague suggests that the guests make their choice by voting. Since there are eight candidate operas, he further suggests that the fairest result will be achieved by giving each guest eight votes to allocate among the operas however he or she wishes. A guest may give all eight votes to one opera, or split votes among his or her top choice and second choice, or split the votes among several operas. From the clues below, can you determine what opera received the most total votes, and who voted how many times for each one?

1. All the guests used all the votes that they were entitled to cast (eight apiece).
2. One guest cast all eight votes for one opera, another cast votes for six different operas, and the others split their votes among two or three operas.
3. Beth and David gave the same number of votes to their top choice but different numbers of votes to their second choice.
4. Apart from Beth and David, no two guests gave the same number of votes to their top choice.
5. Apart from single votes that Taylor cast for more than one opera, no guest gave the same number of votes to two different operas. One of the operas Taylor voted for was *Aida.*
6. No opera received the same number of votes from two different guests.
7. *Rigoletto* received more votes from David than from Jessica, more from Jessica than from Charles, and more from Charles than from Taylor, who gave it just one vote.
8. Beth gave the same number of votes to *Il trovatore* as Jessica did to *Rigoletto.*
9. Exactly half of the total votes received by *Aida* came from Jessica.
10. One of the operas that Karen voted for was *Carmen,* which ended up with a vote total that was an odd number.
11. David, Karen, and Jessica voted for *Aida, Il trovatore,* and *Les contes d'Hoffman,* respectively, and they gave the same number of votes to each of those three operas.
12. *Tosca* received one vote more than *Aida* and two votes more than *Les contes d'Hoffman.*
13. *Die Walküre* received one fewer vote than *Il trovatore.*

	Aida	Carmen	Die Walküre	Il trovatore	Le nozze di Figaro	Les contes d'Hoffman	Rigoletto	Tosca
Beth	0 1 2 3 4 5 6 7 8	0 1 2 3 4 5 6 7 8	0 1 2 3 4 5 6 7 8	0 1 2 3 4 5 6 7 8	0 1 2 3 4 5 6 7 8	0 1 2 3 4 5 6 7 8	0 1 2 3 4 5 6 7 8	0 1 2 3 4 5 6 7 8
Charles	0 1 2 3 4 5 6 7 8	0 1 2 3 4 5 6 7 8	0 1 2 3 4 5 6 7 8	0 1 2 3 4 5 6 7 8	0 1 2 3 4 5 6 7 8	0 1 2 3 4 5 6 7 8	0 1 2 3 4 5 6 7 8	0 1 2 3 4 5 6 7 8
David	0 1 2 3 4 5 6 7 8	0 1 2 3 4 5 6 7 8	0 1 2 3 4 5 6 7 8	0 1 2 3 4 5 6 7 8	0 1 2 3 4 5 6 7 8	0 1 2 3 4 5 6 7 8	0 1 2 3 4 5 6 7 8	0 1 2 3 4 5 6 7 8
Frank	0 1 2 3 4 5 6 7 8	0 1 2 3 4 5 6 7 8	0 1 2 3 4 5 6 7 8	0 1 2 3 4 5 6 7 8	0 1 2 3 4 5 6 7 8	0 1 2 3 4 5 6 7 8	0 1 2 3 4 5 6 7 8	0 1 2 3 4 5 6 7 8
Jessica	0 1 2 3 4 5 6 7 8	0 1 2 3 4 5 6 7 8	0 1 2 3 4 5 6 7 8	0 1 2 3 4 5 6 7 8	0 1 2 3 4 5 6 7 8	0 1 2 3 4 5 6 7 8	0 1 2 3 4 5 6 7 8	0 1 2 3 4 5 6 7 8
Karen	0 1 2 3 4 5 6 7 8	0 1 2 3 4 5 6 7 8	0 1 2 3 4 5 6 7 8	0 1 2 3 4 5 6 7 8	0 1 2 3 4 5 6 7 8	0 1 2 3 4 5 6 7 8	0 1 2 3 4 5 6 7 8	0 1 2 3 4 5 6 7 8
Taylor	0 1 2 3 4 5 6 7 8	0 1 2 3 4 5 6 7 8	0 1 2 3 4 5 6 7 8	0 1 2 3 4 5 6 7 8	0 1 2 3 4 5 6 7 8	0 1 2 3 4 5 6 7 8	0 1 2 3 4 5 6 7 8	0 1 2 3 4 5 6 7 8
Total Votes								

Scavenger Hunt

Early Sunday morning, the Montagues and their staff placed seven sand dollars—each bearing the name of one of the seven guests—at each of five different locations on the island. Beginning at noon, after assembling in front of the mansion, the guests will try to find all five sand dollars bearing their name and be the first to bring them back to the mansion. Of course, everyone is honor-bound not to disturb the other guests' sand dollars during the hunt.

Instead of wandering around the island and potentially wasting time going to distant locations that have no sand dollars, the guests may choose first to try to determine the five correct locations by solving a puzzle that Gordon has prepared, which reads as follows:

Where Are the Sand Dollars?

The five locations for the sand dollars were chosen at random from among these 10 places: the boathouse, the bridge, the cottage, the lighthouse, Lookout Point, the mansion, the old hut, the old well, the pond, and the windmill. Sand dollars are in red containers that are in plain sight at each location. (If the mansion is one of the locations, they will be found in the small game room.)

Below are six pairs of statements. Within each pair, one statement is true and the other is false. Either the true statement or the false statement may come first. Together, the six pairs of true-and-false statements are sufficient to determine the five locations where you'll find the sand dollars.

Pair 1:
There are sand dollars at the cottage but not the windmill.
There are sand dollars at both the cottage and the windmill.

Pair 2:
There are sand dollars at both the pond and the cottage.
There are sand dollars at the old well.

Pair 3:
There are sand dollars at both the lighthouse and the pond.
There are sand dollars at both the bridge and Lookout Point but not at the boathouse.

Pair 4:
There are sand dollars at exactly one of the following locations: the boathouse, the pond, and the windmill.
There are sand dollars at exactly one of the following locations: the bridge, the old hut, and the old well.

Pair 5:
There are sand dollars at exactly two of the following locations: the lighthouse, the mansion, and the pond.
There are sand dollars at exactly two of the following locations: the bridge, Lookout Point, and the windmill.

Pair 6:
There are no sand dollars at any of the following locations: the lighthouse, the mansion, and the pond.
There are no sand dollars at any of the following locations: the bridge, Lookout Point, and the windmill.

Birdwatching

The seven guests (Beth, Charles, David, Frank, Jessica, Karen, and Taylor) are gathered at the customary Friday evening dinner. Gordon addresses the group: "Early this morning Nina, Nolan, and I went birdwatching. We had identified five good places for seeing some interesting species, and each of us visited three of these places. We observed a total of 19 species, each of which could only be seen at one of the five locations. Each of us spent time at just three of the five locations, so we did not all see the same birds."

Nina continues: "Tomorrow we'd like each of you to go birdwatching as we did. Pick three of the five good birdwatching spots—Duck Island, Lookout Point, North Hill, the pond, and the windmill—and try to observe the same species we did. In the library you'll find a checklist of the 19 species to look for, as well as bird books and binoculars. When you return, please give your checklists to Gordon or me."

By late Saturday morning each guest had visited three of the five locations. Gordon and Nina used the information on each guest's checklist to create the following puzzle. From the clues below, can you determine which bird species were observed by each guest, and the location where each species was seen?

1. Of the 10 people who went birdwatching—Gordon, Nina, and Nolan on Friday, and the seven guests on Saturday—no two visited exactly the same set of three locations, and no two ended up seeing the same number of species.
2. The same bird species were present at the same locations both Friday and Saturday, and every guest successfully observed every possible species at each location he or she visited.
3. There was at least one species at each of the five locations, and no two locations had the same number of species.
4. Of the 19 total species the guests were observing, the fewest species seen by a guest was 6, and the most was 16. On Friday Gordon saw 10 species, Nina 11, and Nolan 13.
5. More guests saw a great blue heron than a bluebird, and only three guests saw an osprey.
6. Charles and Jessica were the only guests not to visit the pond.
7. Beth and Taylor were the only guests not to visit the windmill.
8. Beth, David, and Jessica each saw a killdeer.
9. All the guests except Frank, Karen, and Taylor saw a ring-necked pheasant at North Hill.
10. Both Beth and Jessica saw a pelican.
11. At one location guests saw a bluebird, a laughing gull, a red-winged blackbird, and a roseate tern.
12. At one location guests saw an eastern meadlowlark, a great blue heron, a hummingbird, and a pair of mallard ducks.
13. Mourning doves were seen by Beth, Frank, Jessica, and Taylor, but not by the other three guests.

14. The only two guests to see both an indigo bunting and a woodpecker were Beth and Jessica; the only guest to see both a purple martin and a woodpecker was Charles; and the only guest to see both an indigo bunting and a purple martin was Taylor.

15. The only species seen by both Jessica and Karen was a screech owl.

16. The indigo bunting was not seen at Lookout Point, but it was in the same location as the yellow warbler.

17. The white ibis and the pelican were in different locations.

18. More species were seen at Duck Island than at North Hill.

	Beth	Charles	David	Frank	Jessica	Karen	Taylor	Duck Island	Lookout Point	North Hill	pond	windmill
bluebird												
eastern meadowlark												
great blue heron												
hummingbird												
indigo bunting												
killdeer												
laughing gull												
mallard duck												
mourning dove												
osprey												
pelican												
purple martin												
red-winged blackbird												
ring-necked pheasant												
roseate tern												
screech owl												
white ibis												
woodpecker												
yellow warbler												
Duck Island												
Lookout Point												
North Hill												
pond												
windmill												

Total species

In the Big Game Room

The seven guests spent a couple of hours in the big game room, which is so named not because of its size but because of the kinds of games it contains. Along the walls are a pinball machine, several vintage video arcade games, and a tabletop hockey game. In the center of the room is a pool table.

The Montagues organized the guests' big game room activities into six 20-minute periods. They also arranged for two single-elimination tournaments—one in eight-ball pool, the other in tabletop hockey—to be played at the same time. In each of the six periods, one pair of guests played a game of eight-ball while two other guests played a game of tabletop hockey. The three guests not involved in a tournament game during a period each selected one of the pinball or video arcade game machines (Asteroids, Baffle Ball, Defender, Pac-Man, Qix, and Space Invaders) and spent the period playing that by themselves. No guest played on the same game machine in more than one period.

In the first three periods, three different pairs of players met in each tournament. In the fourth period, the player who had not yet played in a tournament played the winner of the period 1 game; in period 5, the winners of the periods 2 and 3 games met; and in period 6, the two remaining undefeated players met to decide the tournament winner. The tournament brackets are shown below.

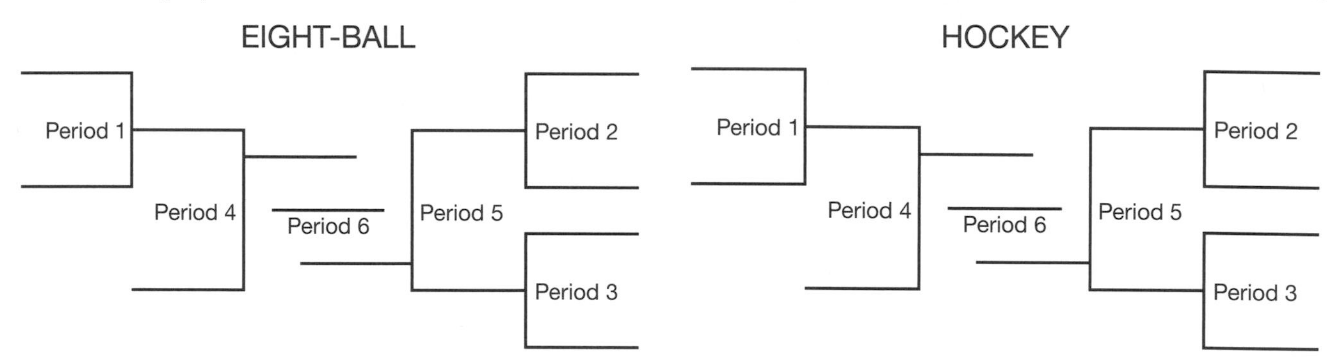

From the following set of facts, can you determine who played what game each period and who won each tournament?

1. One guest only played one game machine, Qix, and played eight-ball before playing hockey.
2. One guest played Defender and later played Asteroids.
3. One guest played Space Invaders two periods before playing Pac-Man.
4. One guest played Asteroids, Pac-Man, and Baffle Ball, in that order, and played eight-ball before playing hockey.
5. One guest played Asteroids, Qix, and Defender, in that order, and played eight-ball before playing hockey.
6. One guest played Baffle Ball two periods after playing Space Invaders but two periods before playing Defender.
7. One guest played Baffle Ball, Space Invaders, Pac-Man, and Qix, in that order, and played eight-ball before playing hockey.
8. The game machines played in period 1 were Asteroids, Baffle Ball, and Space Invaders.

9. The game machines played in period 2 were Asteroids, Pac-Man, and Space Invaders.
10. The game machines played in period 3 were Baffle Ball, Defender, and Qix.
11. The game machines played in period 4 were Pac-Man, Qix, and Space Invaders.
12. The game machines played in period 5 were Baffle Ball, Defender, and Pac-Man.
13. The game machines played in period 6 were Asteroids, Defender, and Qix.
14. Of the two finalists in each tournament, the loser was the one who had been eliminated from the other tournament more recently.
15. David played the most games in the two tournaments combined, while Beth played the fewest.
16. Karen beat David in eight-ball but lost to him in hockey.
17. Jessica lost to Frank in hockey but defeated him in eight-ball.
18. Charles played David only once.

	Qix	Defender, Asteroids	Space Invaders, Pac-Man	Asteroids, Pac-Man, Baffle Ball	Asteroids, Qix, Defender	Space Invaders, Baffle Ball, Defender	Baffle Ball, Space Invaders, Pac-Man, Qix
period 1							
period 2							
period 3							
period 4							
period 5							
period 6							
Beth							
Charles							
David							
Frank							
Jessica							
Karen							
Taylor							

Football Fans

The Montagues are hosting a picnic to mark the arrival of football season. Each guest has two favorite college football teams, and all agree to wear at the picnic a jersey from one of their favorite teams and a souvenir cap featuring their other favorite team.

No two guests have a favorite team in common. The team nicknames are Barracudas, Caribou, Condors, Crocodiles, Dingoes, Lizards, Manatees, Pandas, Pumas, Rhinos, Toucans, Vipers, Vultures, and Wildebeests. Each team's uniform has a dominant color, and its souvenir cap matches that color. The colors—black, blue, gold, green, orange, purple, and red—are each the main color of two of the 14 teams.

From the clues below, can you determine the colors of each guest's jersey and cap, as well as which teams each guest's jersey and cap represent?

1. Each guest's cap is a different color from his or her jersey.
2. Karen's jersey and cap match colors worn by the two guests who are wearing green caps.
3. Beth's cap—which is not a Lizards cap—matches the color of David's jersey, and David's cap matches the color of Beth's jersey.
4. Jessica's cap matches the color of Taylor's jersey, and Taylor's cap matches the color of Jessica's jersey.
5. Guests are wearing souvenir caps of the Pandas, Pumas, and Rhinos.
6. Jessica is wearing a gold jersey, and only Charles is wearing a blue jersey.
7. Beth's jersey is not red, and Taylor's is not orange.
8. The teams with orange or purple uniforms are the Barracudas, Pandas, Toucans, and Vultures.
9. The teams with black or blue uniforms are the Caribou, Crocodiles, Manatees, and Pumas.
10. The teams represented by Beth's and Taylor's jerseys and caps are the Caribou, Lizards, Rhinos, and Vultures.
11. The teams represented by Charles's and David's jerseys and caps are the Crocodiles, Dingoes, Pumas, and Vipers.
12. The Condors jersey or cap and the Toucans jersey or cap are being worn by two different guests.
13. The Condors and Vipers have the same color uniforms.

	Beth	Charles	David	Frank	Jessica	Karen	Taylor	black	blue	gold	green	orange	purple	red
Barracudas														
Caribou														
Condors														
Crocodiles														
Dingoes														
Lizards														
Manatees														
Pandas														
Pumas														
Rhinos														
Toucans														
Vipers														
Vultures														
Wildebeests														

	Beth	Charles	David	Frank	Jessica	Karen	Taylor
black jersey							
blue jersey							
gold jersey							
green jersey							
orange jersey							
purple jersey							
red jersey							
black cap							
blue cap							
gold cap							
green cap							
orange cap							
purple cap							
red cap							

A Family Visit

The Montagues have three nieces (Bonnie, Erica, and Teresa), who come to visit for a week along with their spouses (Duncan, Paddy, and Walton, not necessarily in that order). Each couple stays in one of the three special guest rooms (SG1, SG2, SG3) on the mansion's third floor.

One afternoon the three couples play a game of croquet on the lawn near the patio. Each player chose one of six colored croquet balls (red, orange, yellow, green, blue, black) to be maneuvered through a series of wickets to a stake and back. The players continued the game until everyone had finished and obtained a rank of 1 (first to finish) through 6 (last to finish). The Montagues used this game as the basis for a new puzzle with which to challenge the guests.

From the clues below, can you determine the name of each niece's spouse, the guest room in which each couple is staying, the color of the ball each player used, and the order in which the players finished?

1. Bonnie and Teresa finished second and third, in some order.
2. The ball colors of the last two finishers, in some order, were blue and black.
3. The player with the red ball finished ahead of the player with the green ball but behind the player with the orange ball.
4. The only niece to finish the game ahead of her spouse used the orange ball.
5. Teresa is not staying in SG2.
6. The couple in SG3 finished fourth and sixth.
7. Bonnie, Walton, and the player who used the blue ball are staying in three different rooms.
8. Paddy, Teresa, and the player who used the orange ball are staying in three different rooms.

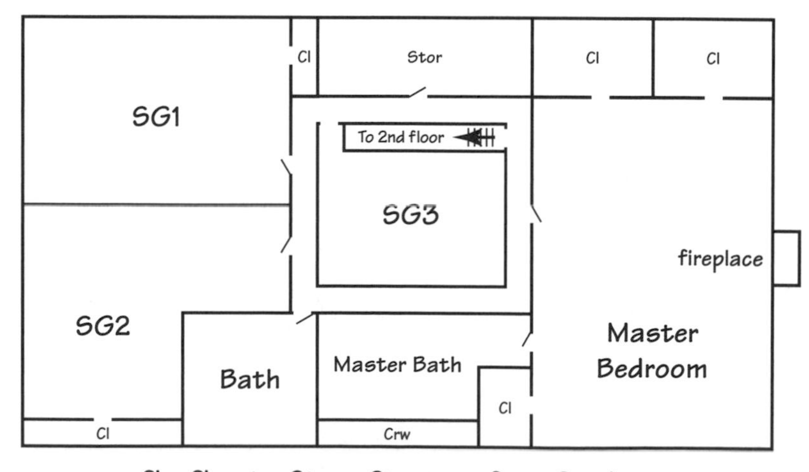

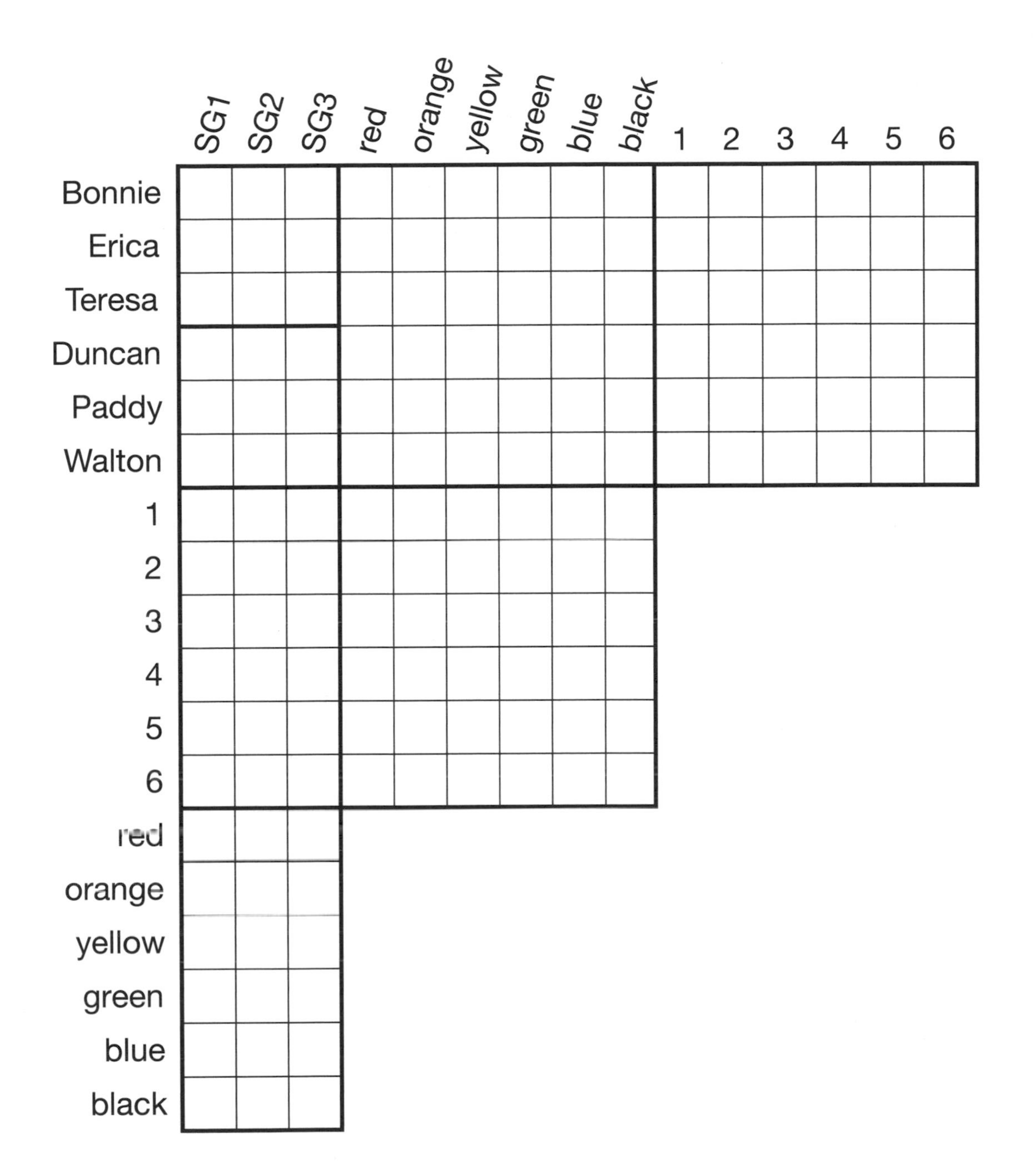
SG1
SG2
SG3
red
orange
yellow
green
blue
black
1
2
3
4
5
6
Bonnie
Erica
Teresa
Duncan
Paddy
Walton
1
2
3
4
5
6
red
orange
yellow
green
blue
black

Incident at the Marina

Saturday afternoon at 1:30, Gordon and Nina Montague went to the boathouse. When they had not returned by 3:00, Alistair went to investigate.

MYSTERY PUZZLE

Instructions for Taylor

In this mystery, you and the other guests are playing the roles of fictitious nephews and nieces of the Montagues. Gordon and Nina were found dead in the marina at 3:15, having apparently drowned after their motorboat crashed into a dock.

Required for a complete solution

Name the killers.

Statement you are to give to other players

I was alone, fishing at the pond, from 12:30 until 3:30. No one else was there. Both David and Karen are in deep financial trouble because they each owe a fortune in back taxes.

Statements by the staff:

1. Alistair: Six of the seven nephews and nieces have serious financial problems. In order to speed up their expected inheritance from the Montagues, three of them staged the boating accident to make the murders of their aunt and uncle look accidental. The guests whose characters are guilty may lie when questioned, but the others may not.
2. Evelyn: The nephew or niece without financial problems, as well as three of the six who have financial problems, are innocent.
3. Grant: Three guests went to the boathouse and marina between 1:30 and 2 this afternoon.
4. Lyle: The three guilty parties met in private Friday evening, two at a time, to discuss their plans. Each conspirator met with each of the other two separately so as not to arouse suspicion.
5. Molly: In separate meetings Friday evening, Beth had private conversations with Frank, Jessica, and Taylor; and Charles, also in separate meetings, had private conversations with David, Frank, and Karen.
6. Sandy: In separate meetings Friday evening, Karen had private conversations with David and Taylor; Taylor also met separately with David and Jessica; and there was a meeting between Frank and Jessica.

Statements by the guests:

7. Beth: I was reading on the screened porch from 1 until 3 this afternoon. No one else was there. Both Frank and Jessica are in deep financial trouble because of large gambling debts.
8. Charles: I was alone, fishing at the pond, from 12:30 until 3:30. No one else was there. Both David and Karen are in deep financial trouble because they each owe a fortune in back taxes.

9. David: I was alone in the library from 1:30 until 3:30 this afternoon. Both Beth and Charles are in deep financial trouble after losing a lawsuit brought against them.
10. Frank: I was alone in the library from 1:30 until 3:30 this afternoon. Both Beth and Charles are in deep financial trouble after losing a lawsuit brought against them.
11. Jessica: I was on a walk to the windmill between 1 and 2 this afternoon, then took a nap in my room. As I came back to the mansion, I saw Beth reading on the screened porch.
12. Karen: I was reading on the screened porch from 1 until 3 this afternoon. Both Frank and Jessica are in deep financial trouble because of large gambling debts.
13. Taylor: I was alone, fishing at the pond, from 12:30 until 3:30. No one else was there. Both David and Karen are in deep financial trouble because they each owe a fortune in back taxes.

SPECIAL ANNOUNCEMENT

Nina addresses the guests on Saturday evening:

"We'll need your help in preparing one of the challenges that will take place on our final puzzle weekend of the year. Between now and then, we want each of you to construct your choice of one of the following types of puzzles: chess problem, crossword puzzle, cryptogram, kakuro, logic puzzle, maze, or sudoku.

"'These puzzles will be the basis for a competition in both making and solving puzzles. We call it 'The Puzzle Game.' Each of you will be given copies of the six puzzles that the other guests made, and you will be allotted 30 minutes per puzzle to solve them. You will earn 1 solving point for each puzzle you solve. You will also earn 1 construction point for each guest who fails to solve the puzzle you created, *provided* that at least one guest solves your puzzle. If no one solves your puzzle, you will get no points for your puzzle construction—so you want to make your puzzle hard to solve within 30 minutes, but not impossible. The guest with the most total points from solving and construction will win the event."

Gift Exchange

Prior to this weekend, each guest visited a different nautical-themed gift shop on the mainland and bought gifts for two other guests. (Each bought both their gifts at the same store.) The gift exchange was planned in such a way that each guest would receive gifts from two other guests, and no one would receive a gift from a guest to whom he or she gave a gift. From the following clues, can you determine who gave what to whom, and at which shop each gift was bought?

1. Frank gave gifts to Beth and Jessica, and Charles received gifts from Beth and Karen.
2. Beth received gifts that were bought at the Crow's Nest and Nemo's Nauticals.
3. David received gifts that were bought at Davy Jones's Locker and Pirates' Cave.
4. Karen received gifts that were bought at Aquatic Crafts and Sailors' Luck.
5. Taylor received gifts that were bought at Octopus's Garden and Sailors' Luck.
6. The model schooner and seashell mosaic came from the same gift shop.
7. The Atlantic Ocean chart and wooden ship wheel came from the same gift shop.
8. The glass pink flamingo and the whale bookends came from the same gift shop.
9. The lighthouse place mats and model schooner were not given to the same guest.
10. Neither the mermaid rain gauge nor the Poseidon statuette was a gift from Taylor.
11. The driftwood dolphin, glass pink flamingo, and pirate flag came from Octopus's Garden, Pirates' Cave, and Sailors' Luck, not necessarily in that order.
12. The coral reef jigsaw puzzle, lighthouse place mats, mermaid rain gauge, and Poseidon statuette were the gifts that came from Davy Jones's Locker and Nemo's Nauticals.
13. The gifts received by Karen and Taylor were, in some combination, the anchor-shaped pillow, driftwood dolphin, seashell mosaic, and whale bookends.
14. Charles, Frank, and Jessica shopped at Nemo's Nauticals, Octopus's Garden, and Sailors' Luck, not necessarily in that order.
15. The guest who received the fisherman's cap gave the glass pink flamingo to the guest who shopped at Sailors' Luck.
16. The fisherman's cap was bought at Pirates' Cave by the guest who gave the pirate flag to the guest who shopped at Aquatic Crafts.
17. The guest who shopped at Octopus's Garden gave a gift to the guest who shopped at Davy Jones's Locker.
18. The guest who was given the anchor-shaped pillow gave the Atlantic ocean chart to the guest who also received the mermaid rain gauge.

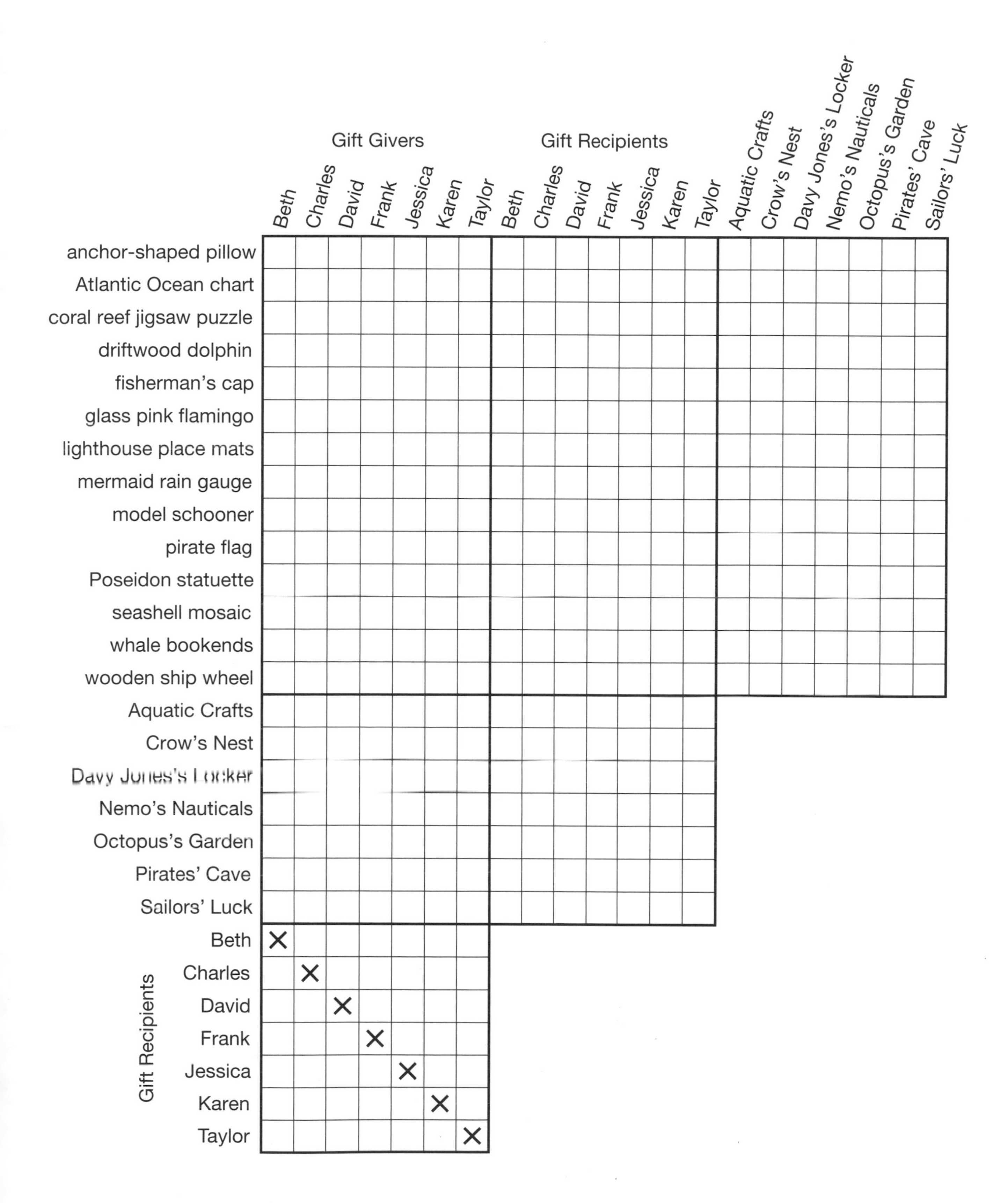
Gift Givers
Beth
Charles
David
Frank
Jessica
Karen
Taylor
Gift Recipients
Beth
Charles
David
Frank
Jessica
Karen
Taylor
Aquatic Crafts
Crow's Nest
Davy Jones's Locker
Nemo's Nauticals
Octopus's Garden
Pirates' Cave
Sailors' Luck
anchor-shaped pillow
Atlantic Ocean chart
coral reef jigsaw puzzle
driftwood dolphin
fisherman's cap
glass pink flamingo
lighthouse place mats
mermaid rain gauge
model schooner
pirate flag
Poseidon statuette
seashell mosaic
whale bookends
wooden ship wheel
Aquatic Crafts
Crow's Nest
Davy Jones's Locker
Nemo's Nauticals
Octopus's Garden
Pirates' Cave
Sailors' Luck
Gift Recipients
Beth
Charles
David
Frank
Jessica
Karen
Taylor

The Puzzle Game

The guests have arrived for the final puzzle weekend of the year. Just after dinner Friday evening, each guest is given copies of the puzzles created by the other six guests as per Nina's instructions of two weeks ago. The guests, spread out in the library and sitting room, begin solving. Every 30 minutes for the next three hours, Nina collects a puzzle from each guest and checks whether it has been correctly solved.

A guest scores 1 point for each puzzle correctly solved. For his or her puzzle construction, a guest scores 1 point for each guest who was unable to solve it. Nina's requirement that a puzzle must be solved by at least one guest to earn any construction points was met by all seven puzzles; each was solved by at least one guest.

As it happens, the seven puzzles the guests chose to construct were all of different types: chess problem, crossword, cryptogram, kakuro, logic puzzle, maze, and sudoku.

From the following clues, can you determine which guest constructed which type of puzzle, which puzzles were solved by each guest, and who won the competition? (Note: Throughout these clues, "solved" means "correctly solved." For each puzzle, a guest either solved it, failed to solve it, or did not attempt it on account of being its constructor.)

1. The total number of points earned by the seven guests for solving puzzles was equal to the total number of points they earned for constructing their puzzles.
2. The guests who constructed the crossword, cryptogram, and kakuro all solved the same number of puzzles.
3. One more guest solved the kakuro than the maze.
4. Charles, David, and Frank constructed the chess problem, logic puzzle, and sudoku, in some order.
5. The number of puzzles solved by Frank was twice the number of guests who solved Frank's puzzle.
6. David solved one more puzzle than Charles.
7. Taylor solved the cryptogram.
8. Only the cryptogram constructor solved the chess problem.
9. The only puzzle solved by both Beth and David was the crossword.
10. Beth and Charles both tried but failed to solve the maze and sudoku.
11. Frank and Taylor both solved the crossword, which was solved by the same number of guests as the sudoku.
12. Frank and Taylor each solved the puzzle the other had constructed.

13. Charles and Karen each solved the puzzle the other had constructed.

14. Beth and Charles had the same number of total points.

15. Frank and Taylor alone tied for the second-most points for puzzle construction.

16. There were two puzzles that both Karen and Taylor solved.

17. There were two puzzles that Jessica and Karen both attempted but failed to solve.

	Constructed							Solved									
	chess	crossword	cryptogram	kakuro	logic puzzle	maze	sudoku	chess	crossword	cryptogram	kakuro	logic puzzle	maze	sudoku	solving points	construction points	total points
Beth																	
Charles																	
David																	
Frank																	
Jessica																	
Karen																	
Taylor																	

Death in the Tool Shed

Saturday at 11:30 A.M. Alistair is found dead in the tool shed by another staff member.

MYSTERY PUZZLE

Instructions for Taylor

In this mystery, the Montagues, their staff, and all the guests are members of a global criminal organization. But one of the guests has a secret.

Required for a complete solution

Name the person who killed Alistair.

Statement you are to give to other players

David and I took a walk between 10 and 10:30. I spent the next hour in the lounge. Frank was in the lounge from 10:30 until 11, and David was in the lounge from 11 until 11:30.

Statements by the Montagues:

1. Gordon: We run an international organization devoted to committing industrial espionage. The guests are all important operatives, gathered here this weekend for an annual planning meeting. Alistair suspected that one of them is working undercover as an investigator from a multinational corporation, and I told him to eliminate that person if he could be sure who it was. Instead, that person killed Alistair in self-defense.
2. Nina: Each guest is from one of the following foreign countries: Australia, Bolivia, China, Denmark, Egypt, France, Germany. No two guests are from the same country. Alistair was sure, as am I, that the guests from Bolivia, China, Denmark, and Egypt are loyal to our organization, and that none of them was the killer. We know that there is only one undercover investigator among the guests, and that person may lie to protect his or her identity. All other guests' statements will be truthful.

Statements by the staff:

3. Evelyn: Frank, Jessica, Karen, and Taylor are from Australia, Egypt, France, and Germany, not necessarily in that order.
4. Grant: I was preparing an area of the greenhouse for some guests who are planning to move some of their garden plants indoors tomorrow. Shortly after 11:30 I went into the tool shed and found Alistair's body next to a hoe. He was holding a knife, and it appeared he had been hit on the head with the hoe.
5. Lyle: There were signs of a brief struggle in the tool shed. Alistair had told me he found a satellite phone hidden in the tool shed and was going to try to catch whoever was using it to secretly communicate with someone off the island.
6. Molly: The guests who were in the lounge from 10 to 10:30 are from Australia and China. The guests in the lounge from 10:30 to 11 are from France and Germany. And the guests in the lounge from 11 to 11:30 are from Denmark and France.

7. Sandy: I saw Alistair at 10:30 as he was going out the front door. He told me that he needed to check on something in the generator shed.

Statements by the guests:

8. Beth: I was in the lounge between 10 and 10:30, as was Jessica. I was alone in my room from 10:30 until 11:30.
9. Charles: I was in my room alone all morning.
10. David: Taylor and I took a walk between 10 and 10:30. After that I went to my room for half an hour, then went down to the lounge and stayed there from 11 until 11:30. Taylor was also in the lounge during that half hour.
11. Frank: I was working in the garden from 11 until 11:30. Jessica and Karen were also there during that time.
12. Jessica: I was in the lounge between 10 and 10:30, as was Beth. I was working in the garden from 10:30 until 11:30. Around 11 I happened to notice Alistair coming out of the generator shed, but I didn't pay attention to where he went next.
13. Karen: I was alone in my room between 10 and 11. After that, I went to the garden and worked there for half an hour. Frank and Jessica were also working in the garden at that time.
14. Taylor: David and I took a walk between 10 and 10:30. I spent the next hour in the lounge. Frank was in the lounge from 10:30 until 11, and David was in the lounge from 11 until 11:30.

	10:00–10:30	10:30–11:00	11:00–11:30	Australia	Bolivia	China	Denmark	Egypt	France	Germany
Beth										
Charles										
David										
Frank										
Jessica										
Karen										
Taylor										
Australia										
Bolivia										
China										
Denmark										
Egypt										
France										
Germany										

The Solving Competition

Nina Montague has everyone's attention as she enters the dining room Sunday morning.

"We are ready to announce the winner of this year's solving competition. We have kept our point awards secret throughout the year until now, and we don't intend to reveal exactly who earned points for what at this time.

"After each of the 12 puzzle weekends, we distributed 100 points, always in multiples of 5, among our seven guests, based on how quickly and accurately they had solved the weekend's puzzle challenges and performed in game tournaments. As it turned out, each guest earned at least 5 points every weekend. We plan to use the competition as the basis for a puzzle that will appear in our book."

The point awards listed at the top of the next page show the number of points that were awarded to each guest each weekend, without indicating which guest got which award. The first weekend's awards are filled in, and the appropriate numbers of points crossed out. The chart at the bottom of the next page shows cumulative point totals of the current point leader at the end of each weekend. Note that every guest led at some point, and the only time there was a tie was after week 11, when there was a four-way tie. Since consecutive numbers are filled in for Beth and Charles, two other weekend point awards that can readily be determined have also been filled in and crossed out.

From the information in the charts and the following clues, can you reconstruct the chart and determine the winner of the solving competition after week 12?

1. Frank received a score of 15 for four consecutive weekends.
2. David and Taylor each received a score of 15 for three consecutive weekends, as well as for weekend 11.
3. David never received the largest point award on any weekend.
4. Jessica received the same number of points in weekend 4 as Karen did.
5. Through weekend 11, Charles, Frank, and Taylor each received the top point total once.
6. Charles received the same number of points six different times—in weekends 3 through 5 and 9 through 11—and he received a different set of three identical point awards in weekends 6 through 8.
7. In weekend 7, Beth received more points than Jessica, and David received more points than Karen.
8. After week 12, Charles had a point total of 105, David had 140, and Karen had 135.
9. Beth's and David's cumulative totals after weekend 5 were the same as Charles's after weekend 6, and their cumulative totals after weekend 8 were the same as Taylor's after weekend 6.
10. Of the four guests who were tied for the lead after weekend 11, the one who had exactly one score of 5 scored 30 points in weekend 12; the guest who never had a 5 scored 25 in weekend 12; the guest who had scored highest in weekend 11 scored 15 in weekend 12; and the other guest who had been tied for the lead scored 10.

Solving Competition Points Awarded Each Weekend

#1	#2	#3	#4	#5	#6	#7	#8	#9	#10	#11	#12
~~25~~	~~25~~	25	25	30	30	30	30	40	35	25	30
~~20~~	20	20	25	25	20	15	15	15	25	15	25
~~15~~	15	15	20	20	15	15	15	15	15	15	15
~~10~~	15	15	15	10	10	10	15	15	10	15	10
~~10~~	10	15	5	5	10	10	10	5	5	15	10
~~10~~	10	5	5	5	10	10	10	5	5	~~10~~	5
~~10~~	5	5	5	5	5	10	5	5	5	5	5

	#1	#2	#3	#4	#5	#6	#7	#8	#9	#10	#11	#12
Beth	25										10	
Charles	10	25										
David	10											
Frank	20											
Jessica	15											
Karen	10											
Taylor	10											

Cumulative Point Totals (Leaders After Weekends 1–11 Are Shown)

	1	2	3	4	5	6	7	8	9	10	11	12
Beth	25									175	185	
Charles	10	35										
David	10		50									
Frank	20					115			155		185	
Jessica	15				90			145			185	
Karen	10			70								
Taylor	10						130				185	

The Secret of the Mansion

"When I asked you to invite my associate to stay in the cottage a few weeks ago, Gordon, I didn't tell you more because I wanted to be sure. When I stayed at the cottage earlier in the year, I searched it carefully and found a door in its basement, concealed behind some shelves. It was locked, and could easily have just been the door to a closet, but it reminded me of the locked doors in one of your mansion's basements. My associate was here to use his special skills to open the locked door in the cottage without making it appear that the lock had been tampered with. He also explored where the door led and placed small, hidden video cameras in three strategic locations that would be activated anytime someone came by."

"And did anyone?" asks Montague.

"Yes. Each of our thieves activated one of the cameras, and from the timing the purpose was clearly to meet and transfer the stamp from the staff member who took it to the guest who would take it off the island."

You hand Gordon Montague a revised floor plan of the mansion's basements.

"As you can see," you explain, "there is a tunnel running from the basement to the cottage. Along the way, it also connects to a crawlspace. If you go into that crawlspace, you will find a ladder that goes up to the first- and second-floor crawlspaces in the wing with the staff quarters. And there's another tunnel that connects to the crawlspace beneath the guest wing, which also has a ladder making it possible to reach any floor. A third crawlspace, in the front of the house, is accessible from the other basement; it divides in two and leads up to the spaces behind the foyer closets as well as the master bath on the third floor."

Montague looks astonished, as you continue.

"Terence Plumly, the former owner of the house, was intrigued by secret passages, ever since he had seen the one in the House of the Seven Gables in Salem, Massachusetts. He had plenty of money at the time, so while renovating the house he built the tunnels and turned every crawlspace into a secret passage that was accessible from panels inside every adjacent closet and storage area. It is possible to reach any crawlspace in the house from any other crawlspace, or from the cottage, without ever going outdoors or using a stairway, making surveillance of those areas useless. The master bedroom can be entered via the crawlspace behind the closet near the master bath, and it's also possible to go from one basement to the other by going through the closets and crawlspace between them.

"My associate placed the cameras near the doors connecting the tunnels to the basement, and also near the entrance to the crawlspace in front that can be used to access the master bedroom.

"One of your staff members has a connection to Plumly, knew all about the secret passages, and had keys to the tunnel doors. This person arranged for an

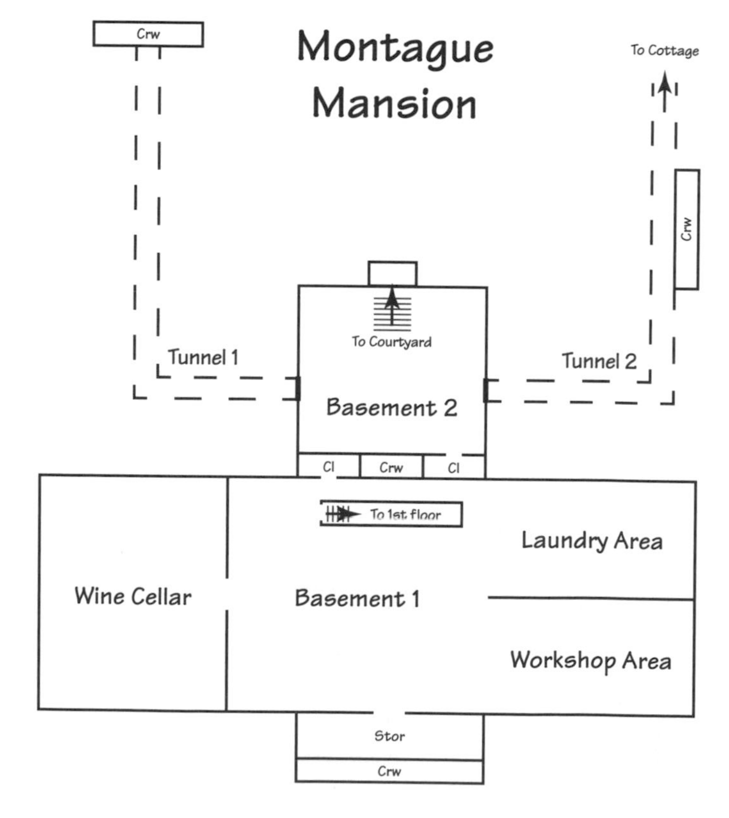

associate to impersonate one of the invited guests last year, and the accomplices were bold enough to repeat the charade this year.

"I'll leave it to you to notify the authorities. But I thought you might first enjoy solving a puzzle yourself for a change. I've created one in the style of your mystery puzzles that will let you identify the two guilty parties. In this case, statements by the staff cannot necessarily be believed. But as usual, statements by you and Nina Montague are definitely true."

Statements by the Montagues:

1. Gordon: Alistair is innocent and his statements can be trusted, but one of the other five staff members who live in the mansion is guilty, along with one of the guests.

2. Nina: The statements by the guilty guest and the guilty staff member may or may not be true, but all the other statements are true.

Statements by the staff:

3. Alistair: Either Jessica is innocent or Evelyn and Sandy are both innocent.

4. Evelyn: If Beth is guilty, then so is either Grant or Lyle. If Jessica is guilty, then Grant and Lyle are innocent.

5. Grant: If Molly or Sandy is guilty, then Beth, Charles, and Karen are innocent. If Lyle is guilty, then David, Frank, and Jessica are innocent.

6. Lyle: If Evelyn is guilty, her accomplice is David, Frank, or Jessica.

7. Molly: If Frank is guilty, his accomplice is either Sandy or Evelyn. If Karen is guilty, her accomplice is Grant or Lyle; but if David is guilty, Grant and Lyle are innocent.

8. Sandy: If Charles is guilty, then so is either Grant or Lyle. If Grant is guilty, then David, Frank, and Jessica are innocent.

Statements by the guests:

9. Beth: If Evelyn is guilty, then David and Frank are innocent. If Molly is guilty, then David and Jessica are innocent.

10. Charles: If Sandy is guilty, then David and Frank are innocent.

11. David: If Beth is guilty, her accomplice is not Grant or Lyle. If David is guilty, his accomplice is not Evelyn or Sandy.

12. Frank: If Grant or Lyle is guilty, then Beth and Karen are innocent. If Molly is guilty, then her accomplice is Beth, Charles, or Karen.

13. Jessica: If Grant or Lyle is guilty, then Charles and Karen are innocent.

14. Karen: If Charles is guilty, his accomplice is either Evelyn, Molly, or Sandy. If Frank is guilty, Evelyn and Sandy are innocent.

	Evelyn	Grant	Lyle	Molly	Sandy
Beth					
Charles					
David					
Frank					
Jessica					
Karen					

Note: Throughout these answers, numbered statements in the puzzles are referred to as "clues."

Weekend 1

Puzzle 1.1: Meet the Guests

Seat 1: David, from Texas
Seat 2: Taylor, from Florida
Seat 3: Beth, from Montana
Seat 4: Frank, from Wisconsin
Seat 5: Jessica, from California
Seat 6: Charles, from New York
Seat 7: Karen, from Kentucky

The left-handed guests are David and Karen.

From clue 1, the left-handed guests are in seats 1 and 7. From clue 2, the guest from Montana must be in seat 3, which is the only seat next to two right-handed guests, and must also be right-handed. Guests from Florida and Wisconsin occupy seats 2 and 4, in some order.

From clues 2, 3, and 5, the left-handed guests can only be from Kentucky and Texas.

From clue 6 and the known positions of the left-handed guests, Charles must be right-handed, and he and the guest from Florida must be in seats 2 and 6, in some order. But since from clue 2 Florida can only be in seats 2 or 4, Florida must be in seat 2, Charles must be in seat 6, and the guest from Wisconsin must be in seat 4.

From clue 7, Frank and the guest from California—since both are right-handed (per clues 3 and 4)—must be in seats 4 and 5, in some order. But since the guest from Wisconsin occupies seat 4, California must be in seat 5 and seat 4 must be Frank's. The only remaining place the right-handed New York guest can be is in seat 6, which means that he is Charles.

Since Jessica is right-handed and sat on the opposite side of the table from Frank (clue 4), she must be in seat 5. Taylor, being right-handed and not from Montana (clue 3), must be from Florida and in seat 2.

From clue 8, Beth and the guest from Texas sat on the same side of the table, and so must be in seats 3 and 1, respectively. Karen must be sitting in seat 7 (and therefore is left-handed) and is from Kentucky, and David is the Texan in seat 1.

Puzzle 1.2: True-False Test

Beth has a club and a spade.
Charles has a diamond and a heart.
David has a diamond and a spade.
Frank has a club and a heart.
Jessica has a heart and a spade.
Karen has two clubs.
Taylor has two diamonds.

Beth, David, and Jessica each have a spade no matter which of their statements is true. Since this accounts for all three spades, the true statements by Charles, Frank, and Karen are the ones that do not mention spades.

If Jessica's first statement were true, her second statement would be as well; therefore, her first statement is the false one, and so her other card must be a heart. Since Charles, Frank, and Jessica each have a heart, all the hearts are accounted for and Beth's second statement is false, so her other card is a club. David's first statement must be false (for the same reason as Jessica), so his other card is a diamond.

Karen's true statement is that she has no diamonds, and so her two cards can only be clubs. Taylor's two cards of the same suit must be the other two unaccounted-for diamonds.

Puzzle 1.3: The Missing Painting

Karen is the thief, and the painting's location is the lighthouse.

The guests' occupations and starting locations are as follows:

Beth, banker, windmill
Charles, gerontologist, cottage
David, entrepreneur, pond
Frank, filmmaker, mansion
Jessica, composer, boathouse
Karen, decorator, lighthouse
Taylor, attorney, garden

Clue 2 (Nina's statement) specifies five possible locations for the painting: the boathouse, cottage, lighthouse, mansion, or windmill.

Both David (clue 11) and Karen (clue 14) state that the painting is not in the boathouse. At least one of them must be telling the truth, since there is only one guilty party (clue 1); therefore, the painting is not in the boathouse.

The painting can only be in the mansion if the entrepreneur is guilty (clue 4). But if the entrepreneur is guilty, then Karen, being the decorator (clue 6), would be innocent and would be telling the truth when she says that the painting is not in the mansion (clue 14); therefore, the painting cannot be in the mansion.

The painting cannot be in the windmill, because if Beth (clue 9) is lying, then Taylor's statement (clue 15) would mean that Jessica is also guilty.

Clues 3 and 7 together mean that the attorney, banker, composer, and decorator started, in some order, at the boathouse, garden, lighthouse, and windmill, since the other three guests started at the remaining locations. From clue 10, Charles the gerontologist, if he is truthful, could only have started at the cottage, in which case the painting is not there (clue 5). But clue 8 states that if Charles is guilty, the painting is also not in the cottage; since it is not in the cottage in either situation, the lighthouse is its only possible location. Karen is lying about the painting's location and is the thief, which means that the statements by all the other guests are truthful.

The remaining occupations and starting locations can be determined as follows:

As given in their statements, Beth is a banker and started at the windmill, and Charles is a gerontologist who, as noted above, must have started at the cottage. Taylor is the attorney and started in the garden (clue 15).

David did not start at the boathouse (clue 11), Frank is not the entrepreneur (clue 12), and Jessica did not start at the mansion or pond (clue 13). Since the painting is in the lighthouse, neither David (clue 11) nor Jessica (clue 13) started there, which leaves the boathouse as Jessica's only possible starting place.

The only places the entrepreneur and filmmaker could have started are the mansion and the pond. Therefore, Jessica cannot be the entrepreneur or filmmaker, and must be the composer. Frank must be the filmmaker, and David the entrepreneur. Since the entrepreneur did not start at the mansion (clue 12), he started at the pond, and Frank started at the mansion. Karen started at the lighthouse (that part of her statement was true).

Weekend 2

Puzzle 2.1: The Guest Rooms

Beth is in room 2A.
Charles is in room 3E.
David is in room 2B.
Frank is in room 1C.
Jessica is in room 1B.
Karen is in room 3D.
Taylor is in room 1A.

From clue 2 and the fact that there are seven guests, there are two floors with two guests each and one floor with three guests.

From clue 3, Beth, David, Jessica, and Taylor occupy rooms with letters A and B, the only rooms with adjoining closets. From clue 4, two of the rooms 1C, 2C, 3C, and 3E are occupied; and because of clues 3 and 4, these can only be occupied by Charles and Frank. Therefore, the D room mentioned in clue 8 must be occupied by Karen, and this can only be 3D, which means that 3E is also occupied.

Since the other guests do not occupy A or B rooms, Beth, David, Jessica, and Taylor must, in some combination, occupy two pairs of adjoining rooms—1A and 1B, 2A and 2B, or 3A and 3B; otherwise, clue 3 could not be true for all four of these guests. They cannot be on the third floor, since the guests in 3D and 3E would make a total of four; this would leave three guests for the other two floors, contradicting clue 2. Therefore, Beth, David, Jessica, and Taylor are in 1A, 1B, 2A, and 2B, in some combination.

Charles and Frank are in 3E and one of the C rooms, in some combination. Since David's room, which is on the first or second floor, is higher up than Frank's (clue 7), Frank must be in 1C, Charles is in 3E, and David is in 2A or 2B.

Since Beth and Jessica are on different floors (clue 8), the one who is on the first floor will pass more guest room doorways before reaching the stairs to the third floor. Since Karen's room is closer to the third-floor stairwell than Charles's, it is not possible for Jessica to pass twice as many guest room doorways in going to Karen's room as Beth does in going to Charles's room unless Jessica is on the first floor. The number of guest room doorways passed in going from 1A to 3D is 10; from 1B to 3D, 8; from 2A to 3E, 4; and from 2B to 3E, 6. Jessica is therefore in room 1B and Beth in 2A. David, then, is in 2B, leaving 1A for Taylor.

Puzzle 2.2: An Evening of Diplomacy

The countries in order of finish, and who played them, are as follows:

1. Austria-Hungary, Frank
2. Russia, Beth
3. England, Taylor
4. Germany, David
5. France, Karen
6. Italy, Jessica
7. Turkey, Charles

Let the numbers 1 through 7 stand for the place that a guest or country finished, from first to seventh. From clues 1 and 2, we know that: Russia did not finish 6 or 7; Germany did not finish 1 or 7; Turkey did not finish 1 or 2; Austria-Hungary did not finish 5, 6, or 7; England did not finish 1, 6, or 7; France did not finish 1, 2, or 7; and Italy did not finish 1, 2, or 3.

From clues 3 and 4, we know that: Beth did not finish 5, 6, or 7; David did not finish 1, 6, or 7; Karen did not finish 1, 2, or 7; Charles did not finish 1, 2, or 3; Frank did not finish 6 or 7; Taylor did not finish 1 or 7; and Jessica did not finish 1 or 2.

From clue 5, David did not finish 2, Russia did not finish 4 or 5 (since it finished four places higher than Italy), and Italy did not finish 4. From clue 6, England did not finish 2, Frank did not finish 4 or 5, and Karen did not finish 3 or 4. Also, since Karen did not finish 7, Frank did not finish 3 (clue 6 means that Frank finished four places higher than Karen) and England did not finish 5. From clues 2 and 3, France did not finish 3 (since England finished no better than 3 but was ahead of France) and Charles did not finish 4 or 5 (since Karen finished no better than 5 and was ahead of Charles).

From clue 7, Germany did not finish 2 or 3, which means that Taylor did not finish 2, and Turkey did not finish 3 or 4 (clue 1). But that means places 1 and 2 can only be filled by Austria-Hungary and Russia, which therefore cannot have finished in any lower places. Similarly, only Frank and Beth can have finished 1 and 2, in some order, and so neither can have finished in any other place.

By elimination, England must have finished 3. From clue 6, Frank finished 1 and Karen finished 5. Beth finished 2.

From clue 5, Italy is four places below Russia and so cannot have finished 7. Thus, Turkey finished 7.

Since Charles must have finished 6 or 7 and Taylor finished ahead of Jessica (clue 4), Taylor cannot have finished 6 with Jessica in 7, since then there would be nowhere for Charles to finish; so Jessica and Charles must have finished 6 and 7, in some order.

From clue 7, Germany can't have finished 6, since Taylor finished no lower than 4. Since France finished better than Italy (clue 2), France cannot have finished 6, so Italy must have done so. From clue 5, David finished 4 and Russia finished 2. Taylor finished 3, and Austria-Hungary 1. From clue 7, since Taylor finished 3, Germany must have finished 4, and so France finished 5.

From clue 8, Jessica must be Italy, finishing 6, and so Charles is Turkey, finishing 7. Since the order of finish of all the countries and all the players is known, it is clear who played which countries.

Puzzle 2.3: In the Library

David is the killer, who lied about the time he was in the library. The guests' subscriptions and times spent in the library are as follows:

Beth: *Feud & Whine*, 3:30–4:30
Charles: *Height Watchers*, 3:30–4:30
David: *Field & Dream*, 2:30–3:30
Frank: *Ferret Fancy*, 1:30–2:30
Jessica: *Courts Illustrated*, 2:30–3:30
Karen: *Popular Séance*, 1:30–2:30
Taylor: *Vanity Hair*, before 1:30

Of the three guests who claim to have been in the library from 3:30 to 4:30, only two can be telling the truth (clue 3). Since the killer acted alone (clue 1), the statements of the other four guests can be trusted.

Each guest subscribes to a different magazine (clue 14). Since clue 1 matches a set of four guests to a set of four magazines, the other three guests subscribe to the other three magazines.

If Charles subscribes to *Popular Séance*, then Karen subscribes to *Height Watchers* (clue 5); but then Nina's first statement (clue 2) cannot be true. Thus, Charles does not subscribe to *Popular Séance*.

If Taylor subscribes to *Ferret Fancy*, then Jessica subscribes to *Courts Illustrated* (clue 6); but then Nina's second statement (clue 2) cannot be true. Thus, Taylor does not subscribe to *Ferret Fancy*.

From the previous two conclusions and clue 7, Jessica subscribes to *Courts Illustrated*.

If Beth subscribes to *Ferret Fancy*, then Taylor subscribes to *Vanity Hair*, according to Evelyn's first statement (clue 4); but then Nina's second statement (clue 2) would be false. Thus, Beth does not subscribe to *Ferret Fancy*, and the only guest who can be that magazine's subscriber is Frank. From Nina's second statement, therefore, Taylor does not subscribe to *Feud & Whine*, which means that Taylor must subscribe to *Vanity Hair* and Beth must subscribe to *Feud & Whine*. From Evelyn's second statement, Karen does not subscribe to *Height Watchers*.

The remaining possible subscribers to *Field & Dream* are Charles, David, and Karen; for *Height Watchers*, Charles and David; and for *Popular Séance*, David and Karen. There is only one combination in which exactly one of the parts of Nina's first statement (clue 2) is true: Charles subscribes to *Height Watchers*, David subscribes to *Field & Dream*, and Karen subscribes to *Popular Séance*.

Since we know that Jessica tells the truth, the person in the library with her from 2:30 to 3:30 was neither Beth nor Charles, who subscribe to *Feud & Whine* and *Height Watchers*. That leaves David as the liar and the murderer.

Weekend 3

Puzzle 3.1: Movie Poll

Jessica's list scored the highest (8). Charles's and David's lists scored 7 each, Karen's scored 5, Taylor's 3, and Beth's and Frank's 2 each.

From clue 1, one film was on three lists and two other films were on two lists each, in order for the total number of listings to add up to 21 (7 lists of 3 titles each).

From clue 2, the scores of the lists must be 2, 2, 8, and a set of four numbers—each greater than 2 but less than 8—that add up to 22, in order to bring the total to 34. These are the possibilities:

3, 5, 7, 7
3, 6, 6, 7
4, 4, 7, 7
4, 5, 6, 7
4, 6, 6, 6
5, 5, 5, 7
5, 5, 6, 6

The only set of numbers consistent with clue 3 is 3, 5, 7, 7; and so, the breakdown of scores is 2, 2, 3, 5, 7, 7, 8.

Call the two movie titles that appear on four lists M4's, the one that appears on three lists M3, the two that are on two lists M2's, and the six that are on one list M1's. (An M4 scores 3, an M3 scores 2, an M2 scores 1, and an M1 scores 0.)

The list that scored 8 points had to include the two M4's and the M3 (scoring 3 + 3 + 2 points). Each of the lists that scored 7 points had to include the two M4's and an M2 (scoring 3 + 3 + 1 points).

Because M4's each appear on four lists, the remaining lists with more than 2 points must each include one of them, and the lists that scored 2 cannot contain any M4's. Therefore, the list with 5 points had to include an M4 and either (i) an M3 and an M1 or (ii) two M2's; and the list with 3 points had to include an M4 and two M1's. Each of the lists with 2 points had to include either an M3 (plus two M1 titles) or two M2's and an M1 title.

From clue 5, neither Frank's list nor Karen's can have scored 7 or 8.

From clue 6, Taylor's list scored 3 and David's 7 (no other pair of possible scores have a difference of 4), and Taylor's list included an M4 movie. This M4 movie must be the one Jessica's and Taylor's lists have in common (clue 4). Jessica's list therefore scored at least 3 points.

From clue 7, Karen's list scored at least 3 points, but since Taylor's list scored 3 and Karen's score cannot be 7 or 8, Karen's list must have scored 5; and since she is known to have listed one M1 (clue 5), her list must also have an M4 and the M3. Since Jessica's list scored at least 3 but cannot have been 3 (Taylor's score) or 5 (Karen's), her list must have scored 7 or 8.

From clue 8, Beth's list cannot have scored 7 or 8, and so Charles's must have, along with David's and Jessica's. Beth's list must have scored 2 and must have included the two unaccounted for M1's (Taylor's list included two M1's, Karen's and Frank's each listed one M1, and none of the lists that scored 7 or 8 had any M1's.) Beth must therefore have scored 2 by listing the M3. Frank's list also scored 2, which he must have achieved by listing the two M2's. The title his list had in common with Charles's (clue 4) had to be an M2, and so Charles's list scored 7, leaving Jessica's as the 8.

In summary, one M4 title was listed by Charles, David, Jessica, and Karen; the other was listed by Charles, David, Jessica, and Taylor. The M3 title appeared on the lists of Beth, Jessica, and Karen. One M2 film was listed by Charles and Frank, and the other by David and Frank. Two M1 films each were listed by Beth and Taylor, and one each by Frank and Karen.

Puzzle 3.2: Uncommon Knowledge

Beth speaks Portuguese and collects decoy ducks.
Charles speaks French and collects classic cars.
David speaks Tagalog and collects baseball cards.
Frank speaks Dutch and collects comic books.
Jessica speaks Spanish and collects souvenir spoons.
Karen speaks Russian and collects perfume bottles.
Taylor speaks Japanese and collects toby jugs.

Clue 1 matches a set of three collections to speakers of three foreign languages, which means that the speakers of the other four foreign languages have the other four collections. Similarly, the four guests not mentioned in clue 2 must speak the four languages not mentioned in clue 2, and the four guests not mentioned in clue 3 must collect the four items not mentioned in clue 3.

Clues 4 through 9 each rule out one connection between a specific language and a specific collection (for example, clue 4 indicates that the Spanish speaker does not collect decoy ducks). Also, these clues provide pairs of statements of which one member is true and the other is false.

The Japanese speaker does not collect baseball cards (clue 6), and since none of the three possible baseball card collectors (clue 3) speak French, the baseball card collector must speak Tagalog. Taylor must therefore collect either baseball cards or toby jugs (clue 9). Jessica must speak either Spanish or Tagalog (clue 7), and is therefore not the toby jug collector. Since neither David nor Taylor speak French, the toby jug collector must speak Japanese.

By elimination, the classic car collector must speak French and is therefore not Beth. Neither David nor Jessica speaks Dutch or Russian, leaving Portuguese and Spanish as the possible languages for the souvenir spoon collector. Because Beth does not collect baseball cards or toby jugs, she does not speak Japanese or Tagalog. From clue 6, David speaks either Japanese or Tagalog, and the same is true of Taylor, who collects either baseball cards or toby jugs. Therefore, none of the others can speak either of these two languages. By elimination, Jessica speaks Spanish and collects souvenir spoons (clue 7), and Beth speaks Portuguese and collects decoy ducks (clue 4).

The comic book collector does not speak Russian (clue 8), and so must speak Dutch. The Russian speaker must collect perfume bottles. Since Frank does not collect classic cars (clue 10), he does not speak French; he doesn't speak Russian either, so he must be the Dutch speaker who collects comic books. Karen therefore speaks Russian (clue 8) and collects perfume bottles, leaving Charles as the French speaker and collector of classic cars. From clue 11, David speaks Tagalog and collects baseball cards, and by elimination, Taylor speaks Japanese and collects toby jugs.

Puzzle 3.3: A Brief Tour

Guests visited the old well in the following order (at the times indicated): Taylor (8:50), Charles (9:00), Karen (9:10), Frank (9:15), Taylor again (9:25), David (9:30), Beth (9:45), and Jessica (10:00).

Taylor, whose path and starting time are known, visited the old well at 8:50 (30 minutes after leaving the mansion) and 9:25 (after spending 10 minutes walking to the sea caves, 15 minutes waiting there, and 10 minutes walking back).

For each of the six different routes the other guests used, calculate how long it takes to reach each location from the mansion. For convenience, call the clockwise path around the northern loop Route 1, the counterclockwise path around the northern loop Route 2, the clockwise path around the southern loop Route 3, the counterclockwise path around the southern loop Route 4, the clockwise path around the outer loop Route 5, and the counterclockwise path around the outer loop Route 6.

Consider clue 5. Only Routes 3, 4, 5, and 6 include Lookout Point. From adding up the appropriate numbers provided by Alistair, the minutes required to reach Lookout Point along these routes are 45, 55, 80, and 55, respectively. Since guests started their walks at 10-minute intervals, someone taking Route 5 could not have arrived at Lookout Point at the same time as anyone taking Routes 3, 4, or 6. But a guest taking Route 3, and who started 10 minutes later than a guest following Route 4 or Route 6, would have met that Route 4 or 6 guest at Lookout Point 45 minutes later. Therefore, David must have taken Route 3 and Jessica took either Route 4 or Route 6.

From the fact that David took Route 3, we know that he reached the pond 20 minutes after leaving the mansion. The times that it takes to reach the pond via the other routes are 75 minutes for Route 1, 20 minutes for Route 2, and 80 minutes for Route 4. Only the person taking Route 4 can reach the pond at the same time as David, and only if that person left the mansion exactly 60 minutes before David. Thus, Karen took Route 4 and left the mansion at 8:00, and David left at 9:00; they met at the pond at 9:20. Jessica must have taken Route 6 and left at 8:50, reaching Lookout Point at 9:45, the same time as David did.

The remaining routes, taken in some combination by Beth, Charles, and Frank, take the following total amounts of time to complete: Route 1, 95 minutes; Route 2, 95 minutes; and Route 5, 135 minutes. The starting times unaccounted for so far are 8:10, 8:30, and 8:40. There are two ways for Frank to have arrived back at the mansion 10 minutes after Beth: (1) by taking Route 1 or 2 and starting at 8:40, while Beth started at 8:30 and took Route 2 or Route 1; or (2) by leaving 30 minutes earlier than Beth and taking Route 5, which is 40 minutes longer than Route 1 or 2.

Reaching the old well takes the following amounts of time for each route: Routes 1 and 5, 65 minutes each; Routes 2 and 3, 30 minutes each; and Routes 4 and 6, 70 minutes each. Adding these times to the possible starting times, we find that if Beth started at 8:30 and Frank started at 8:40, Charles would have left at 8:10 and taken Route 5, reaching the old well at 9:15. To have arrived there later than Charles as required by clue 4, Frank would have to have taken Route 1 instead of Route 2; but in that case, he would also have arrived later than Beth, contradicting clue 5. Therefore, Frank must have left at 8:10 and taken Route 5, arriving at the old well at 9:15. Beth left at 8:40 and must have taken Route 1, since Route 2 would have brought her to the old well before Frank. She reached the old well at 9:35. Charles left at 8:30 and took Route 2, arriving at the old well at 9:00.

For the record, the starting times were: Karen 8:00, Frank 8:10, Taylor 8:20, Charles 8:30, Beth 8:40, Jessica 8:50, and David 9:00.

Puzzle 3.4: Multi-Chess Tournament

Players finished in this order, with the following scores:

1. Frank 6–0
2. Taylor 5–1
3/4. Jessica 3–3
3/4. Karen 3–3
5. Charles 2–4
6/7. Beth 1–5
6/7. David 1–5

From clue 4, one player finished 6–0 and another 5–1. Since they both beat each of the other players, no other player can have finished better than 4–2. From clues 1 and 2, neither of the top two finishers can be David, Charles, or Beth.

From clue 5, since the winner ended up with a 2–0 chess record and the runner-up with 1–1, there must be one player with a chess record of 0–2, with the remaining players all 1–1.

From clue 3, Karen lost at least one game of xiangqi, which means Jessica lost at least one game of shogi (clue 6) Therefore, neither can be the tournament winner or runner-up, since both the winner and runner-up had perfect records in shogi and xiangqi. That means that Frank and Taylor were the ones who played chess in the final round to determine the tournament winner. Therefore, Frank and Taylor won all their games against Jessica, Karen, Charles, David, and Beth.

From clue 3, Frank beat Jessica at chess. From this fact and clues 1, 2, and 3, Taylor must have played Jessica and Beth at shogi, and Frank played Karen and Beth at xiangqi. Since xiangqi games are known to include the pairings Frank–Karen, Frank–Beth, Taylor–Karen, Taylor–Charles, and Jessica–Beth, the remaining xiangqi games must have been David against Jessica and David against Charles.

Since Charles's shogi and xiangqi games are known, his games against Jessica and Karen must both have been chess. Similarly for other players, Jessica vs. Karen must have been shogi, Karen vs. David must have been shogi, and David vs. Beth must have been chess.

Since only the tournament winner (Frank or Taylor) won two chess games and Karen beat Beth at chess, Karen lost the chess game against Charles, and Charles lost the chess game to Jessica.

The player who was 0–2 at chess can only be the loser of the David–Beth chess game. Since Beth is known to have lost five other games and the worst record in the tournament was 1–5 (clue 7), Beth must have won this game.

From clue 6, since Karen was 0–2 in xiangqi (against the players who were undefeated until the final round), Jessica was 0–2 in shogi and so lost that game to Karen. Since Karen beat Jessica at shogi and Jessica beat Beth at xiangqi, then from clue 6, Jessica and Karen either both won or both lost to David at xiangqi and shogi, respectively. But since players Frank, Taylor, Jessica, Karen, and Charles have at least two wins each, only David can be the one who tied for last place with Beth. Therefore, David lost both his games with Jessica and Karen (and his xiangqi game against Charles must be his one win).

From clue 8, the winner was whichever of Frank and Taylor had shogi opponents with the best combined record at shogi. Frank played Charles and David, who ended up 1–1 and 0–2 at shogi; Taylor played Jessica and Beth at shogi, each of whom were 0–2. So Frank won the tournament.

Here was the tournament, round by round. (The order of the rounds could have been different without changing the answer to the puzzle, except that Frank had to have played Taylor in the final round.)

Round 1
chess: Charles vs. Karen (Charles wins)
shogi: Beth vs. Taylor (Taylor wins)
xiangqi: David vs. Jessica (Jessica wins)
bye: Frank

Round 2
chess: Charles vs. Jessica (Jessica wins)
shogi: David vs. Karen (Karen wins)
xiangqi: Beth vs. Frank (Frank wins)
bye: Taylor

Round 3
chess: Beth vs. Karen (Karen wins)
shogi: David vs. Frank (Frank wins)
xiangqi: Charles vs. Taylor (Taylor wins)
bye: Jessica

Round 4
chess: David vs. Taylor (Taylor wins)
shogi: Charles vs. Frank (Frank wins)
xiangqi: Beth vs. Jessica (Jessica wins)
bye: Karen

Round 5
chess: Beth vs. David (Beth wins)
shogi: Jessica vs. Taylor (Taylor wins)
xiangqi: Frank vs. Karen (Frank wins)
bye: Charles

Round 6
chess: Frank vs. Jessica (Frank wins)
shogi: Beth vs. Charles (Charles wins)
xiangqi: Karen vs. Taylor (Taylor wins)
bye: David

Round 7
chess: Frank vs. Taylor (Frank wins)
shogi: Jessica vs. Karen (Karen wins)
xiangqi: Charles vs. David (David wins)
bye: Beth

Weekend 4

Puzzle 4.1: Staff Quarters

Alistair is in S5.
Evelyn is in S1.
Grant is in S3.
Lyle is in S4.
Molly is in S6.
Sandy is in S2.
S7 is unoccupied.

Since Alistair and Evelyn are on different floors (clue 1), as are Sandy and Lyle (clue 3), the occupants of the two first-floor staff rooms must be Alistair and Lyle, Alistair and Sandy, Evelyn and Lyle, or Evelyn and Sandy.

Grant, then, must be on the second floor, so Lyle is too (clue 2) and must be directly above Sandy. Grant and Lyle must occupy S3 and S4, in some order. That leaves either S6 or S7 as Molly's room, with the other of those two rooms unoccupied (clue 4).

From all of the above, the possible combinations are:

Alistair 1, Sandy 2, Grant 3, Lyle 4, Evelyn 5, Molly 6 or 7
Alistair 2, Sandy 1, Grant 4, Lyle 3, Evelyn 5, Molly 6 or 7
Evelyn 1, Sandy 2, Grant 3, Lyle 4, Alistair 5, Molly 6 or 7
Evelyn 2, Sandy 1, Grant 4, Lyle 3, Alistair 5, Molly 6 or 7

Only the third of these, with Molly in S6, is consistent with clue 5.

Puzzle 4.2: Cottage Visitors

The cottage's occupants, in order, were: David, Frank, Taylor, no one, Karen, Beth, Jessica, no one, Charles, no one, Nolan.

From clue 1, the three periods in which the cottage was unoccupied are among the middle nine periods, and no two of them are consecutive. Therefore, the eight guests can be divided into four sets: those who stayed in the cottage before the first unoccupied period, those who stayed between the first and second unoccupied periods, those who stayed between the second and third unoccupied periods, and those who stayed after the third unoccupied period. At least one guest must belong to each set.

From clues 2 and 3, the series of occupants must include the sequences Karen–Beth–Jessica and David–Frank–Taylor; these must be two of the four sets of guests. This leaves only Charles and Nolan, who each must form a set by himself.

From clue 5, the second of the four sets of guests was Karen, Beth, and Jessica. From clue 4, the first of the four sets of guests must be David, Frank, and Taylor; the third set must be Charles; and the final set is Nolan.

Puzzle 4.3: Poisoned

The guilty parties are Beth, who entered the dining room first, and Taylor, who left the room last.

Three facts are stated by the same trio of guests in different combinations of two:

(1) Both Charles and David state that the first two guests to enter the dining room did not include Charles, Karen, or Taylor.

(2) Both Charles and Jessica state that the last two guests to leave the dining room did not include Beth, Frank, or Karen.

(3) Both David and Jessica state that David was not the last guest to leave the dining room.

If any of these three statements is false, two lying guests will immediately be identified. The other two statements would have to be true, since they were spoken by the innocent guest.

If Taylor's statement (clue 14) is true, the second of the above facts is false, which would make Charles and Jessica guilty. It can be shown, however, that in this case the other guests' statements cannot all be true, which would mean there is a third guilty party, contradicting clue 1. Consider Beth's statement (clue 8). For it to be true, either Jessica was the first person to enter the dining room or David was the last guest to leave (or both). If David was the last guest to leave, then David is a liar; while if Jessica was the first person to enter the dining room, then the statement of either Frank or Karen (whichever one got the order of departure of Charles and David wrong) is also untrue.

Taylor, then, is lying. By similar logic, if Beth's statement were true, either David and Jessica would both be lying (about David not being last to leave); or Jessica would be lying (since the first to arrive is guilty) and either Frank or Karen would be lying (about the Charles/David order). Since Taylor is known to be guilty, neither of these possibilities can be correct, and Beth is lying. The true statements state that Taylor didn't arrive first and Beth didn't leave last, so it's the other way around.

Puzzle 4.4: Garden Plots

Beth: plots L (cucumbers) and N (green beans)
Charles: plots H (asparagus) and M (peppers)
David: plots J (carrots) and K (peas)
Frank: plots A (broccoli) and E (squash)
Jessica: plots F (tomatoes) and I (potatoes)
Karen: plots B (lettuce) and C (radishes)
Taylor: plots D (cabbage) and G (turnips)

From clues 2, 3, and 4, plots E, G, and H all border plots used by Charles, Frank, and Taylor. Since no plot borders all three of the plots E, G, and H, and no pair of adjacent plots—except for pairs that include E, G, or H—border all three of the plots E, G, and H, the guests who planted E, G, and H must be, in some order, Charles, Frank, and Taylor.

Since E borders both of Taylor's plots, E cannot be Taylor's plot. One each of Jessica's and Taylor's plots border both E and H; those plots can only be F and G. Since Jessica's plot is not G, hers must be F and Taylor's must be G. Taylor's other plot must be adjacent to both E and G, and so it must be D. Since H borders both of Jessica's plots and her other plot must be adjacent to F, Jessica's other plot must be I.

B and C must be used by the same guest, and from clue 2 that guest must be Karen. Both of David's plots are adjacent to Taylor's plot G, and so David's plots must be J and K, since if they were K and L, J could not be adjacent to its user's other plot. L must be the plot of Beth's that G borders, and N is her other plot. Of Charles and Frank, one of them uses A and E and the other uses H and M.

Clues 6, 7, 8, and 9 identify four places in the garden where a pair of plots both border a pair of other plots and all four plots are used by different guests. From the garden diagram and the known ownership of the plots, these locations can only be, in some order: B and H both bordering E and F; E and H both bordering F and G; E and L both bordering G and H; and G and L both bordering H and K. Only plot H comes up in all four sets of four plots, and so asparagus, which is mentioned in all four clues, is in plot H. The two vegetables mentioned only once in the four clues—lettuce and peas—must be in plots B and K, in some order. The two vegetables mentioned twice in the clues—cucumbers and tomatoes—must be in F and L some order. The two vegetables mentioned three times in the clues—squash and turnips—must be in E and G, in some order.

We know the four vegetables in the corner plots (clue 5), so by elimination, plots D, I, and M hold cabbage, peppers, and potatoes, in some order. From clue 10, peppers and potatoes border one another and must be in I and M, and so plot D contains cabbage. Plots I and M both border H, so H can't be Frank's (clue 10), which means Frank's plots are A and E, and Charles's are H and M. Green beans, one of the four corner plot vegetables (clue 5), borders peppers (clue 10), so must be in N. In clue 11, the plot of Jessica's that borders the corner plot radishes cannot be I, since N is green beans, and must be F, which means that I is potatoes, C is radishes, and M is peppers. Since David's plots (J and K) do not contain broccoli or lettuce (clue 12), J contains carrots and K contains peas; by elimination, broccoli is in A and lettuce is in B. And since David's plots do not border squash or tomatoes (clue 12), G contains turnips, L contains cucumbers, E contains squash, and F contains tomatoes.

Weekend 5

Puzzle 5.1: A Hand of Poker

Flop: ♠K, ♣7, ♣6
Turn: ♥7
River: ♣4

Beth had the best hand before the flop, with a pair of queens. After the flop, the only way that Taylor could have had a better hand than Beth is if the ♣6 turned up in the flop (the other 6's are accounted for). For Charles to have had a better hand than Beth after the flop, a king had to be part of the flop, specifically the ♠K (since no flop cards were red). For Jessica to have been ahead of David, the ♣7 or ♣4 had to have turned up as well, giving her a pair.

After the turn, Jessica moved up to second place, so she must have made three of a kind. This means that the turn card matched either a 7 or 4 in the flop, giving Taylor a full house. Charles still had kings up (two pair, with kings the higher pair), but Beth had queens up, while David, Frank, and Karen each had a pair (of 7's or 4's) and were ranked according to the highest of their other cards.

After the river, Karen is winning, and the only way Karen could beat a full house is with a straight flush. That means the river card was the ♣4 or ♣7. (The ♣2 would be another possibility if it weren't in David's hand.) To beat Taylor's full house that includes three 6's, Jessica must have a full house with three 7's, which means the river card was the ♣4, the ♣7 was part of the flop, and the turn card was the ♥7 (since it's known not to have been a diamond). David ends up with a flush, Frank has a straight, and Charles and Beth still each have just two pair.

Puzzle 5.2: The Lost Goban

Jessica is the thief.

Beth traveled to Abu Dhabi and is the investigator.
Charles traveled to Beijing and is the linguist.
David traveled to Chennai and is the historian.
Frank traveled to Manila and is the magician.
Jessica traveled to Seoul and is the journalist.
Karen traveled to Singapore and is the numismatist.
Taylor traveled to Tokyo and is the knitter.

Clue 3 rules out four guests from being the linguist, magician, or numismatist, while ruling out Charles, Frank, and Karen from having any of the other four occupations.

From clues 2 and 3, the linguist, magician, and numismatist all took their foreign trips two weeks ago. From clue 7, Beth is not the knitter and Jessica is not the historian. Since neither Beth nor Jessica is one of the three who traveled two weeks ago, they must both have traveled three weeks ago (and must be the investigator and journalist in some order), and the knitter and historian both traveled one week ago (and must be David and Taylor in some order).

The investigator traveled the same week as the thief (clue 6), so either Beth or Jessica must be the thief, and everyone else's statements can be trusted, which means Jessica visited either Manila or Seoul (clue 12). Neither the investigator nor the journalist visited Manila (clue 6), so Jessica can't have visited there, and must have gone to Seoul. The investigator didn't travel to Seoul (clue 6), so Jessica is the journalist and Beth is the investigator, which means Jessica is the thief (clue 6) and Beth's statement is true.

Since Jessica didn't travel to Chennai, Beth didn't travel to Tokyo (clue 8), so she went to Abu Dhabi (clue 15), and per clues 9, 10, and 11, Charles went to Beijing, David to Chennai, and Frank to Manila.

Neither the magician nor numismatist traveled to Beijing (clue 5), so Charles must be the linguist. David went to Chennai, so Taylor, traveling the same week, must have visited Tokyo (clue 8), and by elimination, Karen traveled to Singapore. (It turns out that Jessica was telling the truth despite being the thief.) The knitter didn't visit Chennai (clue 4), so David is the historian and Taylor is the knitter. That leaves only the destinations of the magician and numismatist unidentified. The magician must be the one who went to Manila (clue 6), so Frank is the magician, and Karen the numismatist visited Singapore.

Puzzle 5.3: A Relaxing Brunch

Beth had tomato juice, a green chili and cheese omelet, chocolate chip pancakes, an English muffin, and strawberry jelly.

Charles had prune juice, a mushroom and herb omelet, pecan pancakes, wheat toast, and strawberry jelly.

David had orange juice, a jalapeño omelet, chocolate chip pancakes, an English muffin, and strawberry jelly.

Frank had orange juice, a seafood omelet, buttermilk pancakes, wheat toast, and boysenberry jam.

Jessica had orange juice, a seafood omelet, pecan pancakes, an English muffin, and grape jelly.

Karen had grapefruit juice, a seafood omelet, buttermilk pancakes, wheat toast, and strawberry jelly.

Taylor had tomato juice, a green chili and cheese omelet, blueberry pancakes, an English muffin, and red raspberry jam.

Since four guests had strawberry jelly (clue 2) but every food item was chosen at least once (clue 1), the other three jams and jellies were each chosen by only one guest.

Since only one of the three guests who had a seafood omelet had an English muffin (clue 4), and since Beth and Taylor both had English muffins (clue 6), Beth and Taylor did not have seafood omelets. The jalapeño and mushroom and herb omelets were only eaten by one guest each (clue 5) and so both Beth and Taylor must have had the green chili and cheese omelets (clue 6), and that accounts for all seven omelets. From this information as well as clues 4 and 5, we now know that four guests (Beth, Taylor, and from clue 13, David and Jessica) had English muffins and the other three had wheat toast.

Two guests had chocolate chip pancakes and two had pecan pancakes (clue 12), at least two had buttermilk pancakes (clue 10), and at least one had blueberry pancakes (clues 1, 9). Therefore, exactly two guests must have had buttermilk pancakes and only one guest had blueberry. Similarly, since three guests had orange juice (clue 3) and two guests had tomato juice (clue 6), only one guest each had grapefruit juice and prune juice.

Each kind of pancake except blueberry was eaten by one of the three guests who had orange juice (clue 3). Since Frank and the guest who drank grapefruit juice had buttermilk pancakes (clue 10), Frank must be the guest who had orange juice and buttermilk pancakes.

Since Jessica had the same kind of omelet as another guest (clue 8), she must have had a seafood omelet. Since the guest with boysenberry jam had a seafood omelet as well, neither Beth nor Taylor had boysenberry.

Since Charles, Frank, and Karen all had wheat toast, none of them had the jalapeño omelet (clue 5). Since Beth, Jessica, and Taylor had other omelets, the jalapeño omelet must have been David's. Since the four guests who used strawberry jelly had all four kinds of omelets (clue 2), he must have been one of them. David must also have ordered chocolate chip or pecan pancakes, since someone from that group ordered the jalapeño omelet (clue 12).

Since David had strawberry jelly but Jessica did not (clue 2), and they also had different omelets, the category they matched in, which wasn't pancakes, must have been juices (clue 13). Since Beth and Taylor both had tomato juice (clue 6), David and Jessica must have both had orange juice.

Charles had pecan pancakes (clue 11). Since Frank and Jessica both had orange juice, Jessica cannot have had buttermilk pancakes like Frank, nor can she have had the blueberry pancakes (clue 3). Therefore Jessica and David between them had chocolate chip pancakes and pecan pancakes, and so one of them was the second person (along with Charles) who had pecan pancakes, and therefore had grape jelly (clue 11), which means it must be Jessica, since David had strawberry jelly (and therefore David had the chocolate chip pancakes). This means that Beth did not have pecan pancakes, and the only category in which she and Charles can match (clue 14) is jellies and jams. Therefore, they both had strawberry jelly. Since each of the four who had strawberry jelly had a different juice (clue 2), neither Taylor (same juice as Beth) nor Frank (same juice as David) can have been the fourth person who had strawberry, who must therefore be Karen. By elimination, Frank had boysenberry and Taylor had red raspberry.

The four who used strawberry jelly also had four different omelets (clue 2), which means that of Charles and Karen, only one can have had a seafood omelet. This means that for three guests to have had seafood omelets, Frank had to be one of them.

The guest who had grapefruit juice and along with Frank had buttermilk pancakes (clue 10) must be Karen, since Charles had pecan pancakes and the other guests' juices are known. By elimination, Charles had the prune juice and therefore the mushroom and herb omelet (clue 7), and Karen had the other seafood omelet.

Taylor, who we know had red raspberry jam, also had blueberry pancakes (clue 9), which means that Beth had the other chocolate chip pancakes.

Weekend 6

Puzzle 6.1: Kidnapped, Part One

Frank and Jessica are guilty.

The statements by Jessica, Karen, and Taylor all corroborate one another, and only two guests are guilty (clue 2), so the statements must be true and exactly one of those three is guilty (clue 3). One of them must be the guest who told an accomplice that Nina would be taking a walk by herself. The other guilty party must be Beth, Charles, David, or Frank.

If Karen is guilty, David is innocent (clue 6). But David must also be innocent if Karen is innocent, on account of the sets of four guests in clues 4, 5, and 6. Each set contains the name of one guilty party (Beth, Charles, Jessica, Karen in clue 4; Charles, Frank, Karen, Taylor in clue 5; Beth, Frank, Karen, Taylor in clue 6). Karen is the only guest appearing in all three lists, which means that if she is innocent, two other guests among Beth, Charles, Frank, Jessica, and Taylor are guilty. So David is innocent, and the guilty parties must be one of the three guests Beth, Charles, and Frank, and one of the three guests Jessica, Karen, and Taylor. Thus, all two-guest combinations of Beth, Charles, and Frank can be eliminated from consideration as the guilty pair, and the same is true of all two-guest combinations of Jessica, Karen, and Taylor.

Each list of guests in clues 4, 5, and 6 omits David as well as a pair of guests of whom only one is guilty. Thus, the two-guest combinations of Frank and Taylor (clue 4), Beth and Jessica (clue 5), and Charles and Jessica (clue 6) cannot be guilty pairs. Clue 7 eliminates the possible guilty pairs Beth and Karen, Beth and Taylor, Charles and Taylor, Karen and Frank, and Karen and Charles, leaving Frank and Jessica as the only possible guilty pair.

Someone had to have been the person to start the rumor that Gordon wanted Nina to go to the boathouse, yet Beth, Charles, and Frank all claimed to have been given that instruction by someone else. Frank lied when he said he had heard that from another guest.

Puzzle 6.2: Kidnapped, Part Two

Statement 4 is the false one, and B is the location.

Statement 1 is true if the location is B, C, D, E, or F, but false if the location is A or G. That's because its two parts are both true for A and both false for G, whereas exactly one part must be true for the statement as a whole to be true. Through similar reasoning, it can be determined that:

Statement 2 is true for locations A, B, F, and G, but false for C, D, and E.

Statement 3 is true for locations A, B, C, and E, but false for D, F, and G.

Statement 4 is true for locations A and G but false for B, C, D, E, and F.

Statement 5 is true for locations B, E, and F, but false for A, C, D, and G.

Thus, at least two statements are false if the location is anywhere but B.

(While pretending to be kidnapped for much of Saturday, Nina was actually playing cribbage with Nolan in the cabin cruiser.)

Puzzle 6.3: A Cribbage Tournament

The groups and won-lost records in the round-robins were as follows:

Group 1
Jessica (5–1)
Taylor (4–2)
Charles (3–3)
Beth (0–6)

Group 2
Frank (6–0)
Nolan (3–3)
Karen (2–4)
David (1–5)

In the semifinals, Taylor defeated Frank and Nolan defeated Jessica. In the finals, Nolan defeated Taylor.

For eight players to have seven different won-lost records in six games (clue 1), all seven possible records from 6–0 down to 0–6 must have occurred. The two matching records must be 3–3 in order for there to be an equal number of wins and losses.

In each group, the sum of the won-lost records of the players must be 12–12. For a player to finish second with a record of 3–3, as either Charles or Nolan did in Group 2, another player in Group 2 must have scored 6–0, and the others 2–4 and 1–5. Otherwise, there is no way to reach a group total of 12 wins unless another player scores 3–3, which from clue 1 was not the case. It follows that the players' records in Group 1 were 5–1, 4–2, 3–3, and 0–6.

Frank and Taylor finished first or second in their groups (clue 2). From clue 3, Jessica had at least as many wins as Taylor. This means Taylor cannot have 6 wins, and so is not the Group 2 winner. Since the runner-up in Group 2 had 3 wins and must be Charles or Nolan, Taylor must be in Group 1. Frank is therefore in Group 2 and must have had the 6–0 record. That means Taylor was the Group 1 runner-up and Jessica was the Group 1 winner. Since the records of Jessica and Taylor were 5–1 and 4–2, David must have been 1–5 (clue 3). Clue 4 places Karen in Group 2 at 2–4 and Beth in Group 1 at 0–6, and also places Nolan in Group 2 and Charles in Group 1.

The semifinals went to Taylor and Nolan, who had fewer wins than their opponents in the double round-robin, and the finals were similarly won by Nolan.

Weekend 7

Puzzle 7.1: Murder in the Staff Lounge

Charles is the killer, the weapon being a lamp and the motive fear. Weapons and motives were assigned to players as follows:

Beth: candlestick, blackmail
Charles: lamp, fear
David: trivet, revenge
Frank: paperweight, greed
Jessica: bookend, revenge
Karen: vase, anger
Taylor: stone owl, anger

From the statements of Evelyn and Molly, Beth, Karen, and Taylor cannot have the lamp, paperweight, or trivet for a weapon, since those weapons can only go with motives that Beth, Karen, and Taylor are known not to have. From Lyle's statement, Jessica's weapon is also not the lamp, paperweight, or trivet. Therefore, Charles, David, and Frank must have the lamp, paperweight, and trivet as weapons, in some combination, since all seven weapons are assigned to different guests (clue 1).

The statements of Charles, Frank, and Jessica cannot all be true, since the only possible weapon for both Charles and Frank would be the paperweight. One of them is lying and must be guilty, and everyone else's statements are true.

Since David has the same motive as Jessica (revenge, per clue 5), clue 8 rules out David having the lamp as his weapon. David's weapon cannot be the paperweight either, because that would mean Charles and Frank between them have the lamp and the trivet, making two of the statements of Charles, Frank, and Jessica false, which is not possible since only one player is allowed to lie (clue 3). Therefore, David's weapon is the trivet.

By elimination, Charles and Frank are the only ones who can have the weapons lamp and paperweight and the motives fear and greed. From clue 14, Frank's motive must be greed, and so, from clue 8, his weapon is the paperweight. Charles's weapon, then, is the lamp (and his motive is fear). He is therefore the guest who is lying and is guilty.

Since two guests have anger as their motives (clue 10) and each motive is assigned to at least one guest (clue 2), there cannot be a third person with revenge as a motive. Therefore Jessica has the bookend for a weapon (clue 13). Since the guest with the candlestick does not have anger as a motive (clue 10), those with the stone owl and vase must, and the candlestick must go with the motive of blackmail. Karen's weapon is not the candlestick, and she is not the person with the stone owl (clue 14), and so her weapon is the vase. Since Beth does not have the stone owl (clue 8), she has the candlestick and Taylor has the stone owl.

Puzzle 7.2: The Mystery Novels

Beth, 56, is reading *Life on the Nile.*
Charles, 60, is reading *Cards on the Chair.*
David, 48, is reading *Dog Among the Pigeons.*
Frank, 34, is reading *Three-Act Comedy.*
Jessica, 43, is reading *Dead Woman's Folly.*
Karen, 51, is reading *Evil Under the Moon.*
Taylor, 42, is reading *Elephants Can Forget.*

Given that the guests' ages range from 30 through 60, there are only a limited number of ways that one guest's age can be exactly two-thirds, three-quarters, or four-fifths of the age of another guest (clue 7). In particular:

The ⅔ group (number pairs in which the first one is ⅔ the second): 40/60, 38/57, 36/54, 34/51, 32/48, 30/45.

The ¾ group (number pairs in which the first one is ¾ the second): 45/60, 42/56, 39/52, 36/48, 33/44, 30/40.

The ⅘ group (number pairs in which the first one is ⅘ the second): 48/60, 44/55, 40/50, 36/45, 32/40.

One of the ages is 48 (clue 2), so, per clue 7, we can eliminate any pair without a 48 in which one number is one of the ones that has a fractional relationship with 48 (32, 36, and 60). That eliminates 40/60, 36/54, 45/60, 36/45, and 32/40. The set of seven ages will consist of one pair of numbers (all of which must be different) from each group, plus another age that can be found by reversing the digits of one of the other six selected ages (clue 8). The only remaining ages in the above groups that can be reversed while still remaining between 30 and 60 are 34 and 45, in the ⅔ group pairs of 34/51 and 30/45. That means the 48 must come from one of the other two groups, in either the pair 36/48 or 48/60. For those pairs, consider what reversed-digit pair of ages can be added.

(a) 36/48.
The reversed pair can't be 45 and 54, because both numbers have fractional relationships with 36 (36 = ⅘ of 45 and 36 = ⅔ of 54), which would be impossible even if 36 weren't already paired with 48. That leaves 34 (paired with 51) and 43. But then there is no pair in the unused ⅘ group in which both numbers are greater than 48, so clue 2 cannot be fulfilled, and this can't be the correct set of ages.

(b) 48/60.
If the reversed pair is 45 (paired with 30) and 54, we have the ages 30, 45, 48, 54, and 60. Two ages of 50 or less must be one year apart (clue 3), but the only age in the ¾ group one away from 30, 45, or 48 is in the pair 33/44, which would make 48 the third-oldest age instead of the fourth-oldest (clue 2). So the reversed pair is 34 and 43, yielding the partial set 34, 43, 48, 51, 60.

The unused list is the ¾ group, from which a pair must be selected in which one number is less than 48 and the other is larger than 48. 42/56 and 39/52 both fit, and both satisfy the condition that exactly one pair of numbers has a difference of 1. In the case of 39/52, however, the numbers would be 51 and 52, which would contradict clue 3. The guests' ages are therefore 34, 42, 43, 48, 51, 56, and 60. (34 is ⅔ of 51, 42 is ¾ of 56, 48 is ⅘ of 60, and 43 is the digits of 34 reversed.)

Jessica and Taylor must be 42 and 43 years old, in some order (clue 3). The largest difference between adjacent ages in the group is between 34 and 42, so it follows from clue 4 that the three youngest guests are Frank (34), Taylor (42), and Jessica (43). From clues 5 and 10, Taylor is reading *Elephants Can Forget* and Frank is reading *Three-Act Comedy*. Jessica is the unpaired guest in clue 8 who is not reading *Dog Among the Pigeons*. From clue 9, at least Beth, Charles, and Karen are older than the reader of *Dog Among the Pigeons*, and since the three youngest guests are known to be reading other things, the fourth-youngest guest must be reading that book (and, by elimination, must be David). From clue 9, Beth and Charles are the two oldest guests and are therefore reading *Cards on the Chair* and *Life on the Nile* (clue 6). Beth must be the younger of the two (clue 11), so she's reading *Life on the Nile*, and Charles is the oldest, reading *Cards on the Chair*. Karen, the fifth-youngest guest, is not reading *Dead Woman's Folly* (clue 10) so she must be reading *Evil Under the Moon*, and Jessica, by elimination, is reading *Dead Woman's Folly*.

Puzzle 7.3: Mug Shots

Beth has the mug with dots and stars, and drinks three shots of espresso.
Charles has one of the two mugs with stars and triangles, and drinks one shot of espresso.
David has the mug with dots and triangles, and drinks two shots of espresso.
Frank has the mug with diamonds and dots, and drinks decaf coffee.
Jessica has the mug with diamonds and triangles, and drinks two shots of espresso.
Karen has the mug with diamonds and stars, and drinks one shot of espresso.
Taylor has one of the two mugs with stars and triangles, and drinks three shots of espresso.

Six different combinations of two shapes can be made from the four shapes on the mugs, and since there is only one duplicate combination (clue 2), all six combinations can be found among the guests' mugs. The two shapes that appear on the mugs of Charles and Taylor will each appear on four mugs, while the other two shapes will each appear on three mugs.

From clues 1, 3, and 6, both triangles and stars appear on four mugs, which means they are on the mugs of Charles and Taylor.

Since their mugs have stars, Charles and Taylor drink either one or three shots of espresso (clue 6), and so they must be the one-shot and three-shot drinkers among the guests with triangle designs (clue 3). Since Beth drinks more shots than Charles (clue 7), Charles drinks one shot and Taylor three. The other mugs with triangle designs (diamonds-triangles and dots-triangles) are used by guests who each drink two shots (clue 3).

From clue 5, either Beth or Karen must have the mug that features diamonds and stars, and the other must have the one featuring dots and stars. They each must drink either one shot or three (clue 6); but since Beth cannot drink one shot and Karen cannot drink three shots (clue 7), Beth drinks three and Karen one. Karen's mug cannot have dots, since no one with dots drinks just one shot of espresso (clue 4), and so she has the mug with diamonds and stars, while Beth's mug has dots and stars.

By elimination, David, Frank, and Jessica either drink decaf or two shots of espresso. The decaf drinker cannot be using a mug with triangles or stars (clues 3 and 6), and so must be using diamonds and dots. Since there are no diamonds on David's mug (clue 8), he is not the decaf drinker and drinks two shots. He also doesn't drink from the mug with diamonds and triangles, so his mug has dots and triangles. Jessica drinks more shots than Karen (clue 7), so she drinks two shots and uses the mug with diamonds and triangles, leaving Frank as the decaf drinker.

Weekend 8

Puzzle 8.1: Masquerade

One team consists of David (Green Sparrow), Frank (Ironic Man), and Jessica (Chatwoman). The other team is made up of Beth (Stormy), Charles (Incredible Hunk), and Karen (Scarlet Wish).

Each team includes at least one man and one woman (clues 1 and 2). Jessica is not on Beth's team (clue 1). If Beth is Chatwoman, then Karen is Scarlet Wish (clue 6). But in that case, if Karen is on Beth's team, none of the men can be the third teammate (not Incredible Hunk due to clue 3, not Green Sparrow due to clue 4, and not Ironic Man due to clue 5); while if Karen is not on Beth's team, either Incredible Hunk or Ironic Man would have to be, contradicting clue 3 or 5. Therefore, Beth is not Chatwoman.

If Beth is on a team with two of the men (instead of with Karen and one of the men), then she cannot be Stormy (clue 7), but she cannot be Scarlet Wish either; for in that case, neither Green Sparrow (clue 4) nor Ironic Man (clue 5) can be one of her teammates, and so it is not possible to complete her team. Therefore, Beth and Karen must be on the same team. The third member of the team cannot be Frank, since that would mean Charles and David are on the other team, contradicting clue 2. So one team is Beth, Karen, and either Charles or David, and the other team is Frank, Jessica, and either Charles or David.

If Beth and Karen's teammate were David, however, no costume would work for him; he could not be Ironic Man (clue 5) or Incredible Hunk (clue 8) or Green Sparrow (clues 4 and 6). Therefore, Charles is the third member of Beth's and Karen's team.

Since Jessica is not Scarlet Wish (clue 6), either Beth or Karen is, and Charles cannot be Green Sparrow (clue 4). Charles also cannot be Ironic Man (clue 5), which means he is Incredible Hunk. Since Chatwoman is not on the same team as Incredible Hunk (clue 4), Jessica must be Chatwoman.

The remaining choices are: Beth and Karen are Scarlet Wish and Stormy, in some order; and David and Frank are Green Sparrow and Ironic Man, in some order. Clue 9 means that Frank is not Green Sparrow and must be Ironic Man (and David is Green Sparrow), and so clue 10 means that Beth is Stormy (and Karen is Scarlet Wish).

Puzzle 8.2: The Open Safe

Frank, who was in the library, is the thief, since the only other two guests on the first floor around 2 P.M. did not leave the sitting room to go upstairs. The guests' occupations, locations around 2 P.M., and astrological signs are as follows:

Beth, zoologist, lounge, Pisces
Charles, vulcanologist, big game room, Aquarius
David, radiologist, lounge, Libra
Frank, ornithologist, library, Virgo
Jessica, seismologist, sitting room, Taurus
Karen, paleontologist, small game room, Gemini
Taylor, toxicologist, outdoors, Scorpio

From clue 4, the occupations toxicologist, vulcanologist, and zoologist are held by guests with the signs Aquarius, Pisces, and Scorpio; and these are the only three possible occupations for Beth and Taylor, since from clues 3, 5, and 9, neither of them can have the sign Gemini, Libra, Taurus, or Virgo. From clue 12, neither Beth nor Taylor is the vulcanologist; and from clue 11 and the fact that Taylor was outdoors (clue 3), Beth must be the zoologist and Taylor the toxicologist. Since Beth and Taylor both state that they do not have the sign Aquarius, the vulcanologist must have that sign; and from clue 3, Taylor must be Scorpio and Beth Pisces.

From clues 11, 12, and 14, the vulcanologist can only be Charles or Jessica. But Jessica is not the Aquarius (clue 13), and so Charles is the vulcanologist. From clues 5, 6, and 13, he must have been in the big game room around 2 P.M.

Of the signs not yet located, the Gemini and Taurus were not in the library (clue 5), so the guest with the sign Virgo is in the library. This guest is therefore not David (clue 11) or Jessica (clue 13) or Karen (clue 15) and so can only be Frank. The seismologist is not the Virgo and so was not in the library and must have been in the sitting room (clue 3). Since the Taurus was not in the small game room (clue 8), that guest must have been in the sitting room and is the seismologist. By elimination, the guest in the small game room was the Gemini.

Neither David (clue 11) nor Jessica (clue 13) was the person in the small game room, so that must have been Karen. David (not Jessica on account of clue 10) must be the Libra who was in the lounge with Beth (clue 9), so Jessica is the Taurus and the seismologist. Neither Karen nor Frank is the radiologist (clue 15), so David must be.

The thief climbed the stairs (clue 7), so must have been on the first floor, in the library or lounge (clue 3), but Beth and David didn't leave the lounge (clue 9), so Frank is the thief. Frank and Karen are the ornithologist or the paleontologist in some order, but since the paleontologist is innocent (clue 6), Karen must be the paleontologist and Frank is the ornithologist.

Puzzle 8.3: Fifty-Fifty

♥Q ♠7 ♥2 ♣7 ♣A

From the results of the first three guesses, 7 must be one of the answer ranks, as otherwise there would be six different ranks. In the fourth and fifth guesses, the 7 in the fourth position must be correct, for if it were not, the three correct positions in each guess could not be accounted for.

If one of the answer cards is the king, it must be in the third position according to the score for guess #4. In that case, the king in guess #5 must be what earned a 1 for the second digit of the score; and since the 2 could not then be in the correct position, it cannot be in the answer at all, and the two 7's and the ace must be in the correct positions in guess #5. But that contradicts the position of the first 7 in guess #4, which means that there is not a king in the answer.

Since no ranks besides the 7 match in guesses #4 and #5, and each guess has 3 ranks in correct positions, one of the two ranks guessed for each position must be correct (two from each guess). There isn't a king in the answer, so we can determine two more card ranks, giving us _ 7 2 7 _, which leaves us two possibilities: Q 7 2 7 A and 7 7 2 7 3, of which only the first is compatible with the other guesses.

From guess #1, at least one suit is missing from the answer set of cards. From comparing guesses #1 and #2, there must be at least two hearts in the answer but not more than one spade, since replacing a spade with a heart increased the total number of suits present in the guess. From comparing guesses #3 and #4, a spade is present in the answer, but not two diamonds.

Removing the diamonds and adding a spade and a third heart in guess #4 increased the total number of suits found by one. Since a spade is known to be in the answer, the net effect of replacing two diamonds with a third heart was 0, so either there is a third heart and one diamond or there is no third heart and no diamond. A comparison of guesses #4 and #5 shows that a club is present in the answer, which means that there is no room for both a third heart and a diamond. The only remaining possibility is that there is a second club.

The suits are therefore one spade, two hearts, and two clubs. Since only one suit in guess #1 was in the correct position, most possible ways for there to be three correctly positioned suits in guess #4 can be eliminated. Of the heart, club, and spade in positions 2, 4, and 5, at most one can be correct per guess #1, so the hearts in the other two positions in guess #4 must account for the other two correct placements in that guess. That accounts for both hearts, so either the club or spade is correct, but if the spade is correct, then both other positions must contain clubs, making too many matches in guess #1. This leaves heart-spade-heart-club-club as the correct sequence.

Weekend 9

Puzzle 9.1: Popularity Contest

When each guest's rankings are added up, Jessica has the highest total (26), followed by Frank (24), Beth (23), Charles and Karen (19 each), and David and Taylor (18 each).

Let different letters of the alphabet represent the various rankings 1 through 6 until there is enough information to make use of clues 13, 14, and 15. First, look at clue 3. These rankings must all be different values, so assign A to the Beth/Charles rankings, B to the Beth/David rankings, and C to the Charles/David rankings. Now look at clue 2; the rankings given to Jessica can't be A, B, or C (already used by Charles and David), so call them D. As for the two pairs of rankings in clue 4, Beth has already used A and B, and Charles and David have both used C and D, so these must be the two remaining rankings. Assign E to the Beth→Jessica and David→Taylor rankings and F to the Beth→Karen and Charles→Taylor rankings.

The ranking in clue 1 can't be A, B, E, or F (used by Beth) or D (used by Frank), so it's C, and by elimination, Beth assigned Frank a D. From clue 5, Frank gave Charles an A, and so, per clue 2, Frank's ranking of Taylor must be B (Frank has already used A, C, and D, and Charles and David's rankings of Taylor eliminate E and F). According to clue 6, two other guests besides Beth ranked Frank D. Taylor isn't one of those guests, since that clue states Taylor ranked Beth D, and Charles, David, and Frank have already ranked Jessica D, so Jessica and Karen are the ones who ranked Frank D.

The rankings given by Frank to Karen and David in clues 7 and 9 (and their matching rankings) must, by elimination, be E and F in some order. That accounts for the E and F rankings given by Frank, Jessica, Karen, and Taylor, so the four rankings mentioned in clue 8 can only be A (since, by elimination, David only has A and F remaining to assign). That lets us place several rankings by elimination: David ranked Frank F; Jessica ranked Charles B; and Karen ranked Jessica B.

Per clue 10, at least one ranking given to Beth must be F, and that can only be the ranking Beth received from Jessica. This lets us determine which of the rankings mentioned in clues 7 and 9 are E and which are F; clue 9's rankings, which include the Jessica→Beth ranking, are F and clue 7's are E. Per clue 11, Taylor gave Frank a B, and by elimination, gave Jessica a C. Per clue 12, the only way three of the rankings Frank received can match three of Taylor's is if Charles gave him an E (and by elimination, gave Karen a B).

From clues 13, 14, and 15, it follows from inspecting the grid that A = 5, B = 1, C = 4, D = 6, E = 3, and F = 2.

Guests Receiving Rankings

Guests Giving Rankings	Beth	Charles	David	Frank	Jessica	Karen	Taylor
Beth	X	5	1	6	3	2	4
Charles	5	X	4	3	6	1	2
David	1	4	X	2	6	5	3
Frank	4	5	2	X	6	3	1
Jessica	2	1	5	6	X	3	4
Karen	5	2	3	6	1	X	4
Taylor	6	2	3	1	4	5	X

Puzzle 9.2: Murder at the Cottage

Taylor is guilty.

Five guests—Charles, David, Frank, Karen, and Taylor—all gave statements about what time Beth, Frank, and Karen were in the small game room during the morning (either from 8 A.M. until noon, or only until 10 A.M.). Although there is not sufficient information to determine which of these statements is true, it can be shown that only four of the five can be true, as can be demonstrated by considering all possible combinations of Beth, Frank, and Karen either staying in the small game room until noon or leaving at 10 A.M.:

(1) If Beth, Frank, and Karen all left the small game room at 10 A.M., then Charles's statement is false.
(2) If they were all in the small game room until noon, then David's statement is false.
(3) If Karen was not in the small game room until noon but Beth was (regardless of whether or not Frank was), then Frank's statement is false.
(4) If Beth was not in the small game room until noon but Frank was (regardless of whether or not Karen was), then Karen's statement is false.
(5) If Frank was not in the small game room until noon but Karen was (regardless of whether or not Beth was), then Taylor's statement is false.

Since one of the guests making these statements is lying and must be the guilty party, both Beth and Jessica must be innocent, and so their statements can be trusted. Beth's statement proves that Charles and David are innocent, since those who stayed until noon could not have committed the murder. Therefore, the statements by Charles and David can also be trusted. Jessica's statements exonerate both Frank and Karen, since at least one of them must be innocent (clue 3), and that means that the other is as well. All six suspects other than Taylor are therefore innocent, and so by elimination Taylor is guilty. (For the record, this means that Karen stayed in the small game room all morning, Frank left at 10, and Beth may have left at either time.)

Puzzle 9.3: A Night at the Opera

Beth gave 5 votes to *Carmen* and 3 to *Il trovatore*.
Charles gave 6 votes to *Les contes d'Hoffman* and 2 to *Rigoletto*.
David gave 1 vote to *Aida*, 2 votes to *Die Walküre*, and 5 to *Rigoletto*.
Frank gave 8 votes to *Tosca*.
Jessica gave 4 votes to *Aida*, 1 vote to *Les contes d'Hoffman*, and 3 votes to *Rigoletto*.
Karen gave 7 votes to *Carmen* and 1 vote to *Il trovatore*.
Taylor gave 3 votes to *Aida* and 1 vote apiece to *Carmen*, *Die Walküre*, *Le nozze di Figaro*, *Rigoletto*, and *Tosca*.

Carmen received the most votes (13), followed by *Rigoletto* (11), *Tosca* (9), *Aida* (8), *Les contes d'Hoffman* (7), *Il trovatore* (4), *Die Walküre* (3), and *Le nozze di Figaro* (1).

From clues 1, 4, and 5, Taylor cast six votes, some number of which were all 1 votes, with no other repeated numbers, totaling 8. Taylor must have cast at least one vote that wasn't 1. If only four 1 votes were cast, the other two would have to be at least 2 and 3 (to avoid repeats), totaling 9, which is too high. So Taylor's vote allocation pattern is 3–1–1–1–1–1. The other guests voted for, at most, three operas, with no repeated votes, so their top votes must all be 4 or higher. (With a top vote of 3, the maximum total under those constraints is 6.)

Since Beth and David allocated the same number of votes to their top choice but different numbers to their second choice (clue 3), they cannot have allocated 8, 7, or 6 votes to their top choice, since vote allocations of 6–2 and 6–1–1 would contradict clue 5. Nor can they have allocated 4 to their top choices, since it is not possible to have different second choices without also contradicting clue 5 (if one allocated their votes 4–3–1, the other's allocations would have to be 4–2–2). Therefore, Beth and David each gave 5 votes to their top choice, and one must have given 3 to another opera while the other gave 2 votes and 1 vote to other operas. Allocations of votes by the guests other than Taylor are therefore: 8, 7–1, 6–2, 5–3, 5–2–1, and 4–3–1.

From clue 7, Jessica must have given at least 3 votes to *Rigoletto*, Charles gave *Rigoletto* at least 2, and so David gave *Rigoletto* his top allocation of 5. From clue 8 and the above set of vote allocations, the matching vote totals given by Jessica to *Rigoletto* and Beth to *Il trovatore* must be the 3 votes from the 4–3–1 and 5–3 combinations, respectively. Charles therefore gave exactly 2 votes to *Rigoletto* and Taylor gave it a single vote. Beth's voting pattern accounts for one of the top votes of 5, and so David must have allocated his votes in a 5–2–1 pattern. Charles's 2 vote must come from the 6–2 voting pattern.

Among Taylor, Jessica, David, and whoever has the 7–1 pattern, eight single votes were awarded, one of which must go to each opera (clue 6). The three matching votes in clue 11 must all be single votes (since no other numbers appear three times in the voting patterns apart from 3, and two of the 3 votes have already been accounted for). This means that Taylor's five 1 votes were awarded to the other operas: *Carmen*, *Die Walküre*, *Le nozze di Figaro*, *Rigoletto* (as already noted), and *Tosca*. Taylor also voted for *Aida* (clue 5), so *Aida* is the opera that received 3 votes from Taylor.

Since Karen gave 1 vote to *Il trovatore*, she must have the 7–1 voting pattern and Frank is the guest who awarded all 8 votes to one opera. Karen must have given 7 votes to *Carmen* (clue 10).

Aida received 3 votes from Taylor and 1 from David, and so also received 4 votes from Jessica and ended with a total of 8 (clue 9). That means that *Tosca* ended with 9 votes and *Les contes d'Hoffman* with 7 (clue 12).

Carmen received 7 votes from Karen and 1 from Taylor. For *Carmen* to end with an odd number of votes, it must have received Beth's set of 5 votes, bringing its total to 13.

For *Les contes d'Hoffman* to have ended with 7 votes, it must have received 6 votes from Charles, which leaves *Tosca* as the recipient of Frank's 8 votes to complete its total of 9. Since *Il trovatore* received 3 votes from Beth and 1 from Karen, and *Die Walküre* has 1 from Taylor, David must have given 2 votes to *Die Walküre* to account for it having received one vote fewer than *Il trovatore*.

Puzzle 9.4: Scavenger Hunt

The sand dollars are located at the boathouse, the cottage, the lighthouse, the old hut, and the pond.

From pair 1, the cottage must be one of the locations of the sand dollars. From pair 6, we know that the other four locations all are found in one of the following two groups: (i) boathouse, old hut, old well, lighthouse, mansion, pond; or (ii) boathouse, old hut, old well, bridge, Lookout Point, windmill.

The difference between these groups is in the last three locations in each list, which are the sets of locations compared in pair 5. Since exactly two of the three locations are correct in whichever statement in pair 5 is true, the three locations that were in both groups—the boathouse, old hut, and old well—must account for the other two locations. That is, the correct locations are: the cottage; two of the three locations boathouse, old hut, and old well; and two of either (i) the three locations lighthouse, mansion, pond, or (ii) the three locations bridge, Lookout Point, windmill.

If the second statement in pair 3 is true, then neither statement in pair 4 can be true, because if the bridge and Lookout Point are sand dollar locations but the boathouse is not, then the lighthouse, mansion, pond, and windmill are not either—in which case, the five sand dollar locations would have to be the cottage, the bridge, Lookout Point, the old hut, and the old well. Neither statement in pair 4 is consistent with this set of locations. Therefore, the second statement in pair 3 is false, the first statement in pair 3 is true, and the lighthouse and pond are two of the locations with sand dollars. Therefore, in pair 2 the first statement is true, which means that the second one is false and the old well is not a sand dollar location, so the boathouse and old hut are.

Weekend 10

Puzzle 10.1: Birdwatching

Beth, Frank, Jessica, and Taylor visited Duck Island, which had eight species: bluebird, indigo bunting, laughing gull, mourning dove, pelican, red-winged blackbird, roseate tern, and yellow warbler.

Charles, Karen, and Taylor visited Lookout Point, which had two species: osprey and purple martin.

Beth, Charles, David, and Jessica visited North Hill, which had three species: killdeer, ring-necked pheasant, and woodpecker.

Beth, David, Frank, Karen, and Taylor visited the pond, which had five species: eastern meadowlark, great blue heron, hummingbird, mallard duck, and white ibis.

Charles, David, Frank, Jessica, and Karen visited the windmill, which had one species: screech owl.

Beth saw the most species (16), followed by Taylor (15), Frank (14), Jessica (12), David (9), Karen (8), and Charles (6). For the record, Gordon (10) had visited Lookout Point, North Hill, and the pond; Nina (11) had visited Duck Island, Lookout Point, and the windmill; and Nolan (13) had visited Duck Island, Lookout Point, and North Hill.

From the first four clues, the number of species at the five locations must be 1, 2, 3, 5, and 8, for the following reasons. Since one guest saw only 6 species at three locations and no two locations had the same number of species, three of the locations must have 1, 2, and 3 species. To reach the total of 19 species, the number of species at the other two locations must add up to 13. The possibilities are 6 and 7, 5 and 8, or 4 and 9. If they were 6 and 7, it would not have been possible for anyone to have a total of 13 (as Nolan had), as no three numbers in the set 1, 2, 3, 6, 7 add up to 13. If they were 4 and 9, it would not have been possible to have a total of 10 or 11 (as Gordon and Nina had), as no three numbers in the set 1, 2, 3, 4, 9 add up to 10 or 11.

Since no two birdwatchers visited the same set of three locations (clue 1) and the species totals of 2-3-5, 1-2-8, and 2-3-8 are accounted for by Gordon, Nina, and Nolan, respectively, the seven guests visited combinations of locations with species totals of 1-2-3, 1-2-5, 1-3-5, 1-3-8, 1-5-8, 2-5-8, and 3-5-8. Therefore, the location with 1 species was visited by five guests, the location with 2 species by three guests, the location with 3 species by four guests, the location with 5 species by five guests, and the location with 8 species by four guests.

From clues 6 and 7, the pond and windmill were visited by five guests and must therefore be the locations with 1 and 5 species, in some order. From clue 9, four guests visited North Hill, and so it must be the location with 3 species. Since more species were seen at Duck Island than at North Hill (clue 18), and since the location with 5 species is either the pond or the windmill, Duck Island must have 8 species, which means that Lookout Point has 2 species.

From clues 6, 7, and 9, David visited North Hill, the pond, and the windmill, which means he did not visit either Duck Island or Lookout Point. Taylor visited only one of the three locations in clues 6, 7, and 9, and so must have visited both Duck Island and Lookout Point.

Since the mourning dove was seen by four guests (clue 13), it must be at a location with either 3 or 8 species, which are Duck Island and North Hill; but since Frank and Taylor did not visit North Hill, the mourning dove had to be at Duck Island. This means that Beth, Frank, and Jessica were the other visitors to Duck Island. By elimination, Lookout Point was visited by Charles and Karen (as well as Taylor).

Clue 15 indicates that the screech owl is the only species at its location, as otherwise Jessica and Karen would each have seen at least one other species there. It must have been at the windmill, the only place they both visited, which means that the pond is the location with 5 species, and no other species were seen at the windmill.

From clue 14, the indigo bunting cannot be at North Hill, since Taylor saw it, nor at the pond, since Jessica saw it. Clue 16 therefore places the indigo bunting, as well as the yellow warbler, at Duck Island.

The purple martin, seen by Charles and Taylor (clue 14), must be at Lookout Point, the only location they both visited. The osprey must also be at Lookout Point, since it is the only location visited by only three guests (clue 5). Both Lookout Point species are therefore accounted for and it can be eliminated as an option for all other species.

Since Beth, David, and Jessica all saw a killdeer (clue 8), it must be at North Hill, the only location visited by those three guests.

The woodpecker cannot be on Duck Island or the pond since it was seen by Charles (clue 14), so it must be at North Hill. The ring-necked pheasant (clue 9) is the third and final North Hill species, which means that the pelican (clue 10) must be at Duck Island and the white ibis is at the pond (clue 17).

More guests visited the pond than Duck Island, so the great blue heron is at the pond (clue 5), as are the other species mentioned in clue 12. The species listed in clue 11 are at Duck Island.

Puzzle 10.2: In the Big Game Room

Charles won the hockey tournament and Jessica won the eight-ball tournament.

In periods 1, 2, 3, 4, 5, 6, in order, the guests played as follows:

Beth: Baffle Ball, eight-ball (lost), hockey (lost), Space Invaders, Pac-Man, Qix
Charles: Asteroids, Pac-Man, eight-ball (lost), hockey (won), Baffle Ball, hockey (won)
David: eight-ball (won), hockey (won), Qix, eight-ball (lost), hockey (won), hockey (lost)
Frank: hockey (won), eight-ball (won), Defender, hockey (lost), eight-ball (lost), Asteroids
Jessica: hockey (lost), Space Invaders, eight-ball (won), Pac-Man, eight-ball (won), eight-ball (won)
Karen: Space Invaders, hockey (lost), Baffle Ball, eight-ball (won), Defender, eight-ball (lost)
Taylor: eight-ball (lost), Asteroids, hockey (won), Qix, hockey (lost), Defender

The three game machines used each round are known, as is the sequence in which players used game machines. By comparing the two sets of information, the two tournaments can be reconstructed.

Call the guests referred to in clues 1 through 7 players 1 through 7, respectively. (They are also represented, from left to right, by the seven columns in the grid.)

Only player 7 could have played Baffle Ball in period 1. To have played Space Invaders before Pac-Man and Pac-Man before Qix, player 7 must have played Qix in period 6.

It is not possible for a player to play tournament games in all three of the first periods, since the period 3 games are for players who have not yet played in that tournament. Therefore, the person who played Qix in period 4 cannot be player 1, and player 1 must have played Qix in period 3.

The person who played Qix in Period 4 was therefore player 5.

Only Player 2 could have played Asteroids in period 6, since players 3 and 4 played other games after playing Asteroids.

The only time someone played Pac-Man two periods after Space Invaders was in period 4, so it was player 3 who played Space Invaders in period 2 and Pac-Man in period 4. Similarly, player 6 had to be the person who played Space Invaders in period 1, Baffle Ball in period 3, and Defender in period 5. That means that the person who played Space Invaders in period 4 had to be player 7, who must also have played Pac-Man in period 5.

Player 4 had to have played Asteroids in period 1, Pac-Man in period 2, and Baffle Ball in period 5. The person who played Defender in period 3 was player 2, and player 5 played Asteroids in period 2 and Defender in period 6.

We now know when each of the players' tournament games were played, and we know which players' first tournament games were eight-ball. The other players' first games all had to be hockey in order for one game in each tournament to be played each period.

Player 7 lost at eight-ball in period 2 and lost in hockey in period 3.

Player 4 lost at eight-ball in period 3 (since a win would have put player 4 into a period 5 tournament game) but won at hockey in period 4 to reach the finals.

Player 1 won at eight-ball in period 1 and won at hockey in period 2. To have played tournament games in periods 4 through 6, player 1 must have won one game and lost one game in periods 4 and 5 in order to become one of the two finalists in one of the two tournaments.

Player 2 won at hockey in period 1 and won at eight-ball in period 2, but lost at hockey in period 4 and at eight-ball in period 5.

Player 3 lost at hockey in period 1 and won at eight-ball in periods 3 and 5 to reach the finals.

Player 6 lost at hockey in period 2 and won at eight-ball in period 4 to reach the finals.

Player 5 lost at eight-ball in period 1, won at hockey in period 3, and lost in hockey in period 5. Since players 2 and 3 played each other at eight-ball in period 5, player 5 must have lost to player 1 in hockey in that period, which means that player 1 lost at eight-ball in period 4.

Therefore, the eight-ball finalists were players 3 and 6 and the hockey finalists were players 1 and 4. Based on which finalists were most recently eliminated from the other tournament, the tournament winners were players 3 and 4 (clue 14).

Clues 15 through 18 reveal which guests are players 1 through 7. David, who played the most tournament games (5), is player 1; Beth, who played the fewest (2), is player 7. Karen, with the stated record against David, is player 6. Frank and Jessica are players 2 and 3, respectively. Since player 5 played David in both tournaments, player 4 is Charles and player 5 is Taylor.

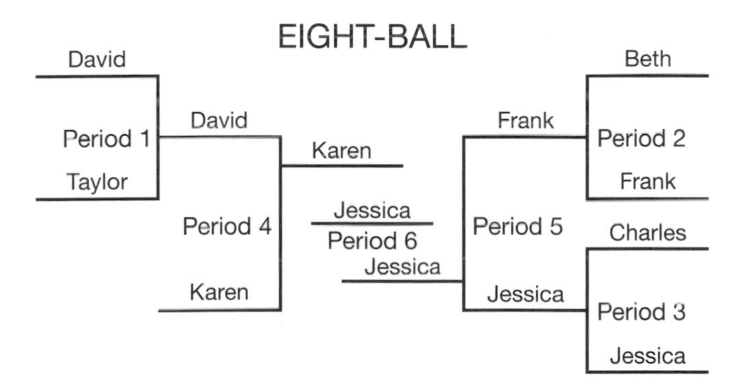

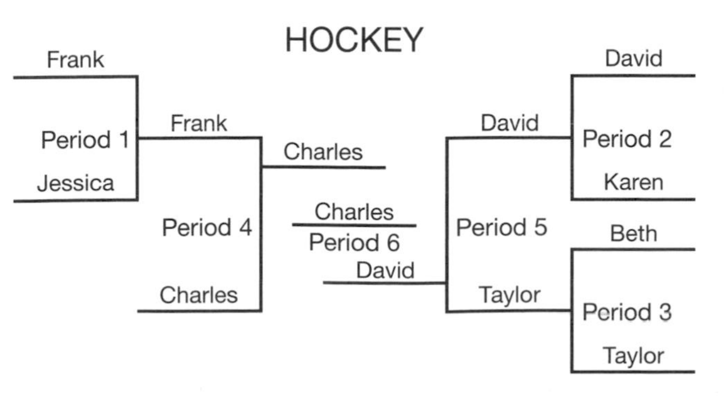

Puzzle 10.3: Football Fans

Beth wears a black Caribou jersey and a red Rhinos cap.
Charles wears a blue Crocodiles jersey and a green Vipers cap.
David wears a red Dingoes jersey and a black Pumas cap.
Frank wears an orange Barracudas jersey and a green Condors cap.
Jessica wears a gold Wildebeests jersey and a purple Pandas cap.
Karen wears an orange Toucans jersey and a blue Manatees cap.
Taylor wears a purple Vultures jersey and a gold Lizards cap.

Since there are only two teams represented by each color (intro), the two guests with green caps in clue 2 are the only guests wearing green, and no one has a green jersey. Karen cannot have a green cap (clue 2); nor can Beth or David, who between them account for all instances of some other two colors (clue 3); nor can Jessica or Taylor, for the same reason (clue 4). Therefore, Charles and Frank have the green caps.

Since Jessica wears a gold jersey (clue 6), Taylor wears a gold cap (clue 4). Since Charles wears a blue jersey and no one else does (clue 6), Karen must have a blue cap to match (clue 2), as well as a jersey of a color matching Frank's jersey.

Since none of David's possible teams listed in clue 11 are among the orange and purple teams listed in clue 8, David wears nothing orange or purple, and since all the blue, gold, and green items are accounted for, the only colors he and Beth can both be wearing are black and red. Since Beth's jersey is not red (clue 7), her cap must be, and so her jersey is black; David's cap must be black, and his jersey red. Taylor's jersey is not orange (clue 7) and can only be purple, which means that Jessica's cap is also purple. Frank and Karen both have orange jerseys.

The colors of the six teams not mentioned in clues 8 and 9 are gold, green, or red. The six teams not mentioned in clues 10 and 11 are all represented by jerseys or caps worn by Frank, Jessica, or Taylor.

Of Beth's four possible teams, only the Caribou can have a black uniform, and so that must be the team represented by Beth's jersey. Similarly, the team on Taylor's purple jersey can only be the Vultures, and the team on Karen's blue cap can only be the Manatees.

Since neither Beth nor David can be wearing an item of the Condors or the Wildebeests, these teams cannot have red uniforms. Because the Condors and Vipers have the same color uniforms (clue 13), the Vipers also cannot be red. This leaves David's only possible red team as the Dingoes.

The Vipers jersey or cap must be worn by Charles or David and must be gold or green in color. Neither Charles nor

David wears gold, and only Charles wears green, so the Vipers are green and worn by Charles. The Condors are therefore also green, and must be worn by Frank. Since both green teams are accounted for, the Wildebeest uniforms cannot be green and can only be gold, which, since they are not one of Taylor's possible teams, means their jersey is worn by Jessica.

Clue 5 resolves most of the remaining uncertainties. The Pandas are orange or purple, and only Jessica's purple cap can be theirs. The Pumas cap must be black and belong to David, and since Beth didn't wear a Lizards cap (clue 3) the Rhinos cap must be red and belong to Beth, which means that the Lizards are gold and their cap is worn by Taylor. Since the same person does not wear both Condors and Toucans clothes (clue 12), Karen wears orange for the Toucans and Frank wears orange for the Barracudas. By elimination, Charles wears a blue Crocodiles jersey.

Weekend 11

Puzzle 11.1: A Family Visit

The couples and their rooms are: Teresa and Walton, SG1; Bonnie and Duncan, SG2; and Erica and Paddy, SG3.

Walton finished first and used the yellow ball.
Bonnie finished second and used the orange ball.
Teresa finished third and used the red ball.
Paddy finished fourth and used the green ball.
Duncan finished fifth and used the black ball.
Erica finished sixth and used the blue ball.

Since the blue and black balls were used by the players who finished fifth and sixth (clue 2), clue 3 means that the orange ball finished first or second, the red ball finished second or third, and the green ball finished third or fourth. Since the orange ball was used by a niece (clue 4), that ball must have finished second, since Bonnie and Teresa are known to have finished second and third in some order, and if Erica used the orange ball to finish first, all three nieces would have finished ahead of their spouses, contrary to clue 4. Therefore the red ball finished third, the green ball fourth, and yellow first. Bonnie and Teresa between them had the red and orange balls. From clue 8, Teresa did not use the orange ball, so Bonnie must have used it and finished second, while Teresa had the red ball and finished third.

Erica cannot have finished fourth, since two of the nieces would then have finished ahead of their spouses. Her ball color is therefore either blue or black, and she must be the niece in the couple who finished fourth and sixth (clue 6), and so is staying in SG3 and finished sixth. Teresa must be in SG1 and Bonnie in SG2 (clue 5).

The player with the yellow ball, who finished first, can't have stayed in SG3 (in which the couple finished fourth and sixth) or in SG2 (where Bonnie, in second place with the orange ball, finished ahead of her spouse), so he is in SG1. From clue 8, since Teresa and Bonnie (the player with the orange ball) are in SG1 and SG2, Paddy must be in SG3 and finished fourth (and therefore has the green ball).

Since the two balls of the couple in SG1 are known to be red and yellow, the player who used blue must be in SG2 or SG3. From clue 7, the blue ball was not used by someone in SG2, so it must belong to Erica in SG3, which also means that Walton must be Teresa's spouse in SG1. By elimination, Duncan is in SG2, used the black ball, and finished fifth.

Puzzle 11.2: Incident at the Marina

Charles, David, and Karen are guilty.

Three pairs of guests give conflicting statements about being alone at a certain location during the time the crime was committed: Beth and Karen, David and Frank, and Charles and Taylor. At least one of each pair must be lying; and since we know there are exactly three killers, the other three are innocent, and Jessica must be innocent as well.

Therefore, Jessica is truthful when she corroborates Beth's statement about being on the screened porch. Karen's statement is a lie, so she is guilty.

Each statement about which guests have financial problems is spoken by two guests, one of whom is known to be innocent, which means the information is true. Since the guest without financial problems is innocent (clue 3), Taylor is innocent, and so Charles is guilty.

The third guilty guest is either David or Frank. Per clues 4, 5, and 6, since David met with both Karen and Charles on Friday night but Frank met only with Charles, David is the third guilty guest.

Puzzle 11.3: Gift Exchange

Beth shopped at Pirates' Cave and bought the fisherman's cap for Charles and the pirate flag for David.

Charles shopped at Octopus's Garden and bought the glass pink flamingo for Jessica and the whale bookends for Taylor.

David shopped at Aquatic Crafts and bought the model schooner for Frank and the seashell mosaic for Karen.

Frank shopped at Nemo's Nauticals and bought the mermaid rain gauge for Beth and the Poseidon statuette for Jessica.

Jessica shopped at Sailors' Luck and bought the anchor-shaped pillow for Karen and the driftwood dolphin for Taylor.

Karen shopped at Crow's Nest and bought the Atlantic Ocean chart for Beth and the wooden ship wheel for Charles.

Taylor shopped at Davy Jones's Locker and bought the coral reef jigsaw puzzle for Frank and the lighthouse place mats for David.

Clue 1 establishes certain donor-donee pairs and also means that (i) neither Beth nor Jessica gave a gift to Frank and (ii) Charles did not give a gift to either Beth or Karen.

Clues 2–5 reveal the pairs of shops that were the source of gifts for four of the guests. Each shop that provided a gift to a guest can be ruled out as the shop where that guest shopped. Clue 14 narrows down the buyer-shop connections further, as no one except Charles, Frank, and Jessica can be the guest who shopped at Nemo's Nauticals, Octopus's Garden, or Sailors' Luck.

Since clue 11 names items that came from three different shops, the same-shop pairs of items in clues 6 and 7 cannot be from any of these shops. From clue 8, the whale bookends must have come from Octopus's Garden, Pirates' Cave, or Sailors' Luck.

Clue 13 reduces to four the possible gifts received by Karen and Taylor and also means that no one else could have received any of these gifts.

The glass pink flamingo was not bought at Sailors' Luck (clue 15). The fisherman's cap and pirate flag were bought by the same guest at Pirates' Cave (clue 16). By elimination, the glass pink flamingo was bought at Octopus's Garden, and so the whale bookends were also bought there (clue 8). The glass pink flamingo cannot have been given to Beth or David (clues 2 and 3), nor to Karen or Taylor (clue 13).

Taylor's gifts came from Octopus's Garden and Sailors' Luck, which, from clue 14 and the fact that Taylor was not one of Frank's recipients (clue 1), must have been shopped at by Charles and Jessica, in some order, which means that Frank shopped at Nemo's Nauticals. Charles cannot be the guest who received the glass pink flamingo, since his gifts came from Beth and Karen, both of whom are known not to have shopped at Octopus's Garden. The guest who received the glass pink flamingo shopped at Sailors' Luck (clue 15), so it isn't Frank, since he shopped at Nemo's Nauticals; therefore, by elimination Jessica received the glass pink flamingo and shopped at Sailors' Luck, and Charles shopped at Octopus's Garden. The other gift from Octopus's Garden, the whale bookends, must have been given by Charles to Taylor, and so Taylor is the guest who shopped at Davy Jones's Locker (clue 17). Charles received the fisherman's cap that came from Pirates' Cave (clue 15).

By elimination (per previous deductions from clues 6, 11, and 13), the anchor-shaped pillow and driftwood dolphin were the two gifts bought by Jessica at Sailors' Luck and given to Karen and Taylor, in some order, and so the seashell mosaic was the gift that Karen received from Aquatic Crafts (clue 4). The other gift from Aquatic Crafts was the model schooner (clue 6).

Of the four gifts that could come from Davy Jones's Locker (clue 12), two were not given by Taylor (clue 10), leaving the coral reef jigsaw puzzle and lighthouse place mats as the gifts Taylor bought at Davy Jones's Locker. By elimination, the mermaid rain gauge and Poseidon statuette are from Nemo's Nauticals, and the Atlantic Ocean chart and wooden ship wheel are from Crow's Nest.

Since Charles received the fisherman's cap, David's gift from Pirates' Cave (clue 3) must be the pirate flag, which makes him the guest who shopped at Aquatic Crafts (clue 16), leaving Beth as the Pirates' Cave shopper and Karen as the shopper at Crow's Nest.

It is now possible to determine which guests gave gifts to which other guests, keeping in mind that no guest gave a gift to a guest from whom he or she received a gift. Beth's gifts went to Charles and David, Charles's gifts went to Jessica and Taylor, and Jessica's gifts went to Karen and Taylor. David did not give Beth a gift (since she gave him one), leaving only Frank and Karen as his possible recipients. Karen did not give David a gift, since he gave her one, so Taylor is the other guest who gave David a gift. Taylor did not give a gift to Beth, since neither of Beth's gifts came from Davy Jones's Locker, and so Karen gave Beth a gift and Taylor gifted Frank.

After eliminating gifts that each guest could not have received because their gifts came from shops that the gift could not be from, it is clear that Karen is the Crow's Nest shopper who was given the anchor-shaped pillow (clue 18), leaving Taylor as recipient of the driftwood dolphin. The Atlantic Ocean chart and mermaid rain gauge can only both go to Beth, who received gifts from both their shops of origin. By elimination, Charles was given the wooden ship wheel, Jessica the Poseidon statuette, and Frank the model schooner. The lighthouse place mats were therefore not given to Frank (clue 9), so they were given to David. The other gift Frank received was the coral reef jigsaw puzzle.

Weekend 12

Puzzle 12.1: The Puzzle Game

(Throughout this solution, "solved" means "successfully solved," and "solver" means "successful solver.")

Beth constructed the kakuro, solved by three guests; Beth solved the crossword, cryptogram, and logic puzzle, for 3 + 3 = 6 points.

Charles constructed the chess problem, solved by only one guest; Charles solved only the cryptogram, for 1 + 5 = 6 points.

David constructed the sudoku, solved by four guests; David solved the crossword and maze, for 2 + 2 = 4 points.

Frank constructed the logic puzzle, which was solved by two guests; Frank solved the crossword, cryptogram, maze, and sudoku, for 4 + 4 = 8 points.

Jessica constructed the crossword, which was solved by four guests; Jessica solved the cryptogram, kakuro, and sudoku, for 3 + 2 = 5 points.

Karen constructed the cryptogram, which was solved by five guests; Karen solved the chess problem, kakuro, and sudoku, for 3 + 1 = 4 points.

Taylor constructed the maze, which was solved by two guests; Taylor solved the crossword, cryptogram, kakuro, logic puzzle, and sudoku, for 5 + 4 = 9 points, winning the game.

The guests attempted to solve a total of 42 puzzles (six per guest), but succeeded in solving only 21, since the solving and construction points were equal (clue 1).

Four crossword solvers are known (clues 9 and 11), which means there had to be at least four sudoku solvers (clue 11). Since these do not include Beth or Charles (clue 10) or whoever constructed the puzzle, there must be exactly four sudoku solvers and four crossword solvers, and the constructors of those puzzles each earned 2 construction points for the two guests who failed to solve those puzzles. The sudoku solvers must include Jessica, Karen, and Taylor, none of whom were its constructor (clue 4).

Taylor did not construct the chess problem, logic puzzle, or sudoku (clue 4); nor the cryptogram, which he solved (clue 7); nor the crossword (clue 11). Taylor therefore did not solve the chess problem (clue 8), which means that Frank did not construct it (clue 12).

Frank did not construct the sudoku, since that was solved by four guests and it is impossible for Frank to have solved eight puzzles as would be required by clue 5 in that case. The only other puzzle Frank could have constructed, in view of clue 4, is the logic puzzle, which Taylor therefore solved. Since Charles tried to solve the sudoku (clue 10), he must have constructed the chess problem, so David constructed the sudoku (and Frank solved it). Karen solved Charles's chess problem and constructed the cryptogram (clues 8 and 13). Since Charles and Karen constructed other puzzles, Jessica—the only other person not to have solved the crossword—was the crossword constructor. That leaves Beth and Taylor as the kakuro and maze constructors in some order. Beth tried and failed to solve the maze (clue 10), so she constructed the kakuro and Taylor constructed the maze (which Frank solved, per clue 12).

Since his chess problem was solved by only one guest, Charles earned 5 construction points. Frank and Taylor were tied for the second-most construction points (clue 15), and they must each have had 4; for if they had only 3 and the remaining guests had even lower totals, the total number of construction points would be fewer than 21.

From clue 3, Beth had 3 construction points. Adding that to the 5, 2, 4, 2, and 4 construction points that were earned by Charles, David (for the sudoku), Frank, Jessica (for the crossword), and Taylor, respectively, yields a total of 20, leaving only 1 construction point for Karen, which means that five guests solved the cryptogram. (And three people solved the kakuro, while two each solved the logic puzzle and maze.)

Since Charles solved the cryptogram (clue 13) and has 5 construction points, his total points must be at least 6. But for Beth's total points to equal his (clue 14), Beth must have solved both the cryptogram and logic puzzle in addition to the crossword to reach the total of 6, and Charles must have solved nothing besides the cryptogram.

Beth and Taylor both solved the logic puzzle, and were the only two to solve it. Since Beth had 3 solving points, so did Jessica and Karen (clue 2). Besides sudoku, the other puzzle that both Karen and Taylor solved must have been kakuro (clue 16), and the two that Jessica and Karen both tried but failed to solve (clue 17) were the logic puzzle and maze. Jessica had to have solved the cryptogram and kakuro to reach 3 solving points, and so neither David nor Frank solved the kakuro. David and Frank were the two solvers of the maze, and Frank had to have solved the cryptogram for his solving total to be 4. Therefore, David did not solve the cryptogram and had 2 solving points.

Puzzle 12.2: Death in the Tool Shed

Jessica is the undercover investigator who killed Alistair in self-defense.

Having discovered a satellite phone hidden in the tool shed, Alistair had been keeping an eye out for anyone entering the shed. When Jessica did so that morning around 10:45, he followed her in, planning to kill her, but she reacted too quickly for him and landed a fatal blow with a hoe.

Since they corroborate each other's statements, Beth and Jessica were in the lounge from 10:00 to 10:30, and David and Taylor were in the lounge from 11:00 to 11:30. Those facts, plus clues 3 and 6, pinpoint the countries of five guests: Beth–China, Charles–Bolivia, David–Denmark, Jessica–Australia, and Taylor–France. Everyone has a corroborated alibi from 11:00 to 11:30 except Beth and Charles, but since they are from China and Bolivia, they are innocent (clue 2).

The murder therefore took place before 11 but after 10:30 (clue 7). We know David is from Denmark and Taylor is from France. Since the guest from Denmark is innocent (clue 2) and the guest from France was in the lounge from 10:30 to 11:30 (clue 6), both are innocent. Taylor's statement that Frank was in the lounge from 10:30 to 11:00 is therefore true, so Frank has an alibi and is from Germany, and by elimination Karen is from Egypt (and innocent, per clue 2). Everyone now has an alibi or is known to be innocent except Jessica, who must be the killer. Her statement that she saw Alistair coming out of the generator shed at 11 was meant to create confusion about the time of death and give herself an apparent alibi.

Puzzle 12.3: The Solving Competition

The guests' points earned each weekend and cumulative points throughout the year are shown in these charts:

Points Awarded for Puzzle Solving Each Weekend

	#1	#2	#3	#4	#5	#6	#7	#8	#9	#10	#11	#12
Beth	25	5	15	5	10	10	15	15	40	35	10	10
Charles	10	25	5	5	5	10	10	10	5	5	5	10
David	10	20	20	5	5	10	15	15	15	5	15	5
Frank	20	10	15	20	20	30	10	15	15	15	15	25
Jessica	15	15	5	25	30	15	10	30	5	10	25	15
Karen	10	10	25	25	5	5	10	5	15	5	15	5
Taylor	10	15	15	15	25	20	30	10	5	25	15	30

Cumulative Point Totals After Each Weekend

	#1	#2	#3	#4	#5	#6	#7	#8	#9	#10	#11	#12
Beth	25	30	45	50	60	70	85	100	140	175	185	195
Charles	10	35	40	45	50	60	70	80	85	90	95	105
David	10	30	50	55	60	70	85	100	115	120	135	140
Frank	20	30	45	65	85	115	125	140	155	170	185	210
Jessica	15	30	35	60	90	105	115	145	150	160	185	200
Karen	10	20	45	70	75	80	90	95	110	115	130	135
Taylor	10	25	40	55	80	100	130	140	145	170	185	215

Since Karen could not have had as many as 50 points after weekend 3, when David led with 50, she must have had 45 at that point and received 25 points in weekend 4, which means that Jessica did as well (clue 4).

Taylor could not have had more than 110 points in weekend 6, since Frank led with 115; so to reach 130 the following weekend, Taylor must have earned 30 points in weekend 7 and had 100 points after weekend 6. This was also Beth's and David's total after weekend 8 (clue 9). For Beth to gain 75 points in weekends 9 and 10, she must have earned 40 points in weekend 9 and 35 in weekend 10.

Since Taylor accounts for the 30-point award in weekend 7, Beth and David each scored 15 points that weekend (clue 7) and the other guests, including Frank, 10 each. Frank's four consecutive weekends of 15 (clue 1) cannot have come by weekend 6, since there was no score of 15 in weekend 5 (and even if there were, scoring four 15's would not have allowed him to reach 115 points by weekend 6). So he must have earned 15 points in four consecutive weekends of the five from 8 through 12, which must include weekends 9, 10, and 11. Frank's score of 10 in week 7 brings his cumulative score to 125, and his score of 15 in week 9 means his score after week 8 was 140, so his fourth 15 score was in weekend 8.

Since Taylor scored 15 points in weekend 11 (clue 2) and therefore had a point total of 170 after weekend 10, Taylor's three consecutive 15's could not have come after weekend 7. Since no one was awarded 15 points in weekend 5, they must have happened in weekends 2 through 4, which means that Taylor had 55 points after weekend 4. To gain 45 more points by weekend 6, Taylor either had to earn 30 points in weekend 5 and 15 in weekend 6, or else 25 points in weekend 5 and 20 points in weekend 6. But Taylor is known to have earned the top award in only one weekend through weekend 11 (clue 5), and that happened in weekend 7; so Taylor earned 25 in weekend 5 and 20 in weekend 6.

We already know Charles scored 10 in weekend 7, so he also scored 10's in weekend 6 and weekend 8 (clue 6). The score that Charles received six times (clue 6) must be a 5, since six 10's plus the 35 points he had after weekend 2 and the three 10's from weekends 6 through 8 would bring him to 125 without including the score from weekend 12, and that's already 20 more than the 105 he actually ended with (clue 8). So Charles scored 5 in weekends 3, 4, 5, 9, 10, and 11. This means his total after weekend 11 was 95, so he received 10 points in weekend 12. It also means that his total after weekend 6 was 60, and Beth and David had this same total after weekend 5 (clue 9). To go from 50 points to 60 points in weekends 4 and 5, David must have earned two 5's.

Taylor had at most 150 points through weekend 9, since Frank led with 155, and so must have earned 25 points on weekend 10 to reach 170. (Scoring 35 isn't possible, because then Taylor's minimum score over weekends 8, 9, and 10 would be 45, bringing the weekend 10 score to 175.) That means Taylor earned a total of 15 points in weekends 8 and 9, which can only have been achieved by earning 10 in weekend 8 and 5 in weekend 9 (when no 10's were awarded).

David never earned the top point award (clue 3); so, in order to reach 50 by weekend 3, he must have earned 20 points each on weekends 2 and 3 instead of 15 on weekend 2 and 25 on weekend 3. This leaves Karen's only way of earning 35 points in weekends 2 and 3 as 10 points in weekend 2 and 25 points in weekend 3.

Jessica had at most 65 points after weekend 4, since Karen led with 70, and so she must have earned 30 points on weekend 5 to reach 90. Since she is known to have earned 25 points in weekend 4, she had 35 points after weekend 3.

Frank had at most 45 points after weekend 3, since David led with 50 then, so Frank earned at least 70 points in the next three weekends. He must therefore have earned 20, 20, and 30 points in weekends 4, 5, and 6, respectively, and he must have had 45 points after weekend 3. To have earned 25 points in weekends 2 and 3, he must have earned 10 points in weekend 2 and 15 in weekend 3.

The only weekend 2 awards not accounted for are for 5 and 15 points, which must go to Beth and Jessica, respectively, since Beth's total must remain below Charles's total of 35 after weekend 2. Jessica also earned 5 points in weekend 3 to reach 35. The remaining weekend 3 award of 15 must be Beth's, as must the remaining award of 5 for weekend 4. This means that Beth earned 10 points in weekend 5 to reach her known total of 60 at that point, and weekend 5's remaining award, a 5, is Karen's.

Since Beth went from a score of 60 after weekend 5 to a score of 100 after weekend 8, and is known to have earned 15 in weekend 7, her scores in weekends 6 and 8 must add up to 25. Since the two 10 scores in weekend 8 are accounted for by Charles and Taylor, Beth must have scored 10 in weekend 6 and 15 in weekend 8. The exact same thing is true of David.

Since the four guests who were leading after 11 weekends scored 30, 25, 15, and 10 points in weekend 12 (clue 10), and since Charles also scored 10 points in weekend 12, David and Karen each scored 5 points in weekend 12.

Jessica must have received 5 points in weekend 9, since Frank was in the lead with 155 at that point, and she could only have reached 185 after round 11 by earning 10 points in weekend 10 and 25 points in weekend 11. Since Jessica earned 10 points in weekend 7 but went from 90 to 145 in weekends 6 through 8, she must have earned 15 points in weekend 6 and 30 in weekend 8.

The two weekend 9 awards and two weekend 11 awards not accounted for are all 15's, which were earned by David and Karen. The remaining awards that are unaccounted for are 5's that went to Karen in weekends 6, 8, and 10, and to David in round 10, and the rest of the cumulative totals through week 11 can be calculated in the chart.

From clue 10 and observation of the completed chart, Taylor earned 30 points to finish in first place with 215 points; followed by Frank, who earned 25 to reach 210 points; then Jessica, with 15 for a total of 200; and Beth, with 10 for a total of 195 points.

Puzzle 12.4: The Secret of the Mansion

Molly and Frank are guilty.

Consider all possible pairs of accomplices consisting of a staff member and a guest. Since Alistair can be trusted, his statement eliminates the possible pairs Evelyn–Jessica and Sandy–Jessica as being accomplices. The other statements by staff and guests eliminate various possibilities, but without certainty since any individual could be lying. But since only one staff member and one guest are guilty, corroboration of a fact by two staff members or by two guests is sufficient to confirm a fact. So, for example, when Evelyn says, "If Beth is guilty, then so is either Grant or Lyle," the pairings Beth–Evelyn, Beth–Molly, and Beth–Sandy can be partially eliminated, subject to corroboration by another staff member.

One solving method is to place an S in a box in the grid to indicate that a staff member has made a statement ruling out that pair, and to place a G in a box to indicate that a guest has made a statement ruling out that pair.

Every pairing but one can be eliminated by statements from two staff members or by statements from two guests. The exception is Molly and Frank, each of whose statements eliminates the Molly–Frank pairing but is never corroborated by anyone else. They must be the guilty pair.

Molly is the granddaughter of Terence Plumly. She visited the mansion many times as a child and had always dreamed of one day living there, but her hopes were dashed when it left her family's possession. She managed to obtain the position of secretary to the Montagues, after which she was able to alter an invitation so that it went to her cousin instead of the intended recipient. "Frank" (not his real name), with keys to the basement doors and information provided by Molly, was able to move through the secret passages at will to replace items of value with counterfeit versions and smuggle them off the island. The two thieves hoped that the missing items would not be discovered for a long time, and "Frank" would eventually just disappear, leaving Molly in the clear and still in a position to steal more items in the future.